yugoslavia

'70

  spektar

  čgp delo

photographers

spektar zagreb   m. babić | m. pfeifer   duško kečkemet author

čgp delo ljubljana   t. dabac | b. turina   jože brumen layout

Ivan Meštrović

by Duško Kečkemet

McGraw-Hill Book Company
New York   London   Toronto   Sydney

My poor,
small homeland.
In my heart
you are greater and dearer
than anywhere else
in the world.

Library of Congress Catalog Card Number: 76-150462
SBN 07-033492-3
Printed in Yugoslavia

1

2

3

It was through the works of Ivan Meštrović that Croatian and Yugoslav art came to be known not only in Europe, but throughout the world. Indeed there was a time when the South Slavs, their past and their hopes for the future, were primarily known through his sculptures.

Long before Meštrović's time whole generations of sculptors, stone-masons and builders had come from Dalmatia, and although this may not always be immediately obvious, their contribution to his creative personality and to his style were enormous.

The life into which Meštrović was born could offer him very little. He came from a region that was not only poor, but had for centuries been a frontier area, infertile, exploited by the Venetians, plundered by the Turks, neglected by the Austrian administration.
The ordinary people had a continual struggle for mere existence. This would hardly seem a suitable place for continuing a tradition, let alone for the rise of a new artistic genius. Only occasional stone fragments carved with the special old interlacing design showed that the ancient Croatian civilization had once flourished in these parts. Such carvings were turned up when the stony vineyards were hoed, or were found by the well loved folk archeologist, Fra Lujo Marun. Then there were the shallow carvings of folk motifs on the peasants' distaffs, fiddles, pipes or wooden jugs. These were all the artistic tradition that the rocky, neglected Dalmatian Alps had to offer. Nevertheless when we are tempted to look for the origins of the rhythm of movement in the hair of Meštrović's Kossovo heroes and widows, or in the mane and tail of the huge horse upon which Kraljević Marko rode in the influence of the Viennese Secession movement, or in the inspiration got in museums from Assyrian or ancient Greek carvings, we must remember that those same decorative elements and rhythm are found in the horses' manes that Meštrović carved as a boy in his own mountains. The rhythm of the folk songs and folk poetry of his childhood and of the old Romanesque Croatian three-band plaited designs played their part too. For those early manes and tails were carved long before Meštrović knew anything about the existence of either Secession or Eastern art.

We must not forget that just below the harsh and naked highlands was the coastal region of Dalmatia with a vital cultural tradition living on unbroken from classical times to Meštrović's own. The monumental palace of the Emperor Diocletian in Split, not far from where Meštrović was born, was an inspiration to centuries of Dalmatian artists and to Meštrović too. The architectural idea behind his *Temple of Kossovo* is that of Split cathedral, which is the mausoleum of a Roman Emperor given a Romanesque belfry. It was the mausoleum, a centrally domed building, that provided the inspiration for his family memorial in his birthplace of Otavice. Another piece of inspiration from Split came from the coffered ceiling of the Temple of Jupiter (now the baptistry) which Meštrović used in the interior of the memorial chapel that he built for the Račić family in Cavtat. The ground-plan of this last, in the from of an equal cross, is taken from the plan on which the Old Croatian churches were built, like that in Nin. The shape of the church he designed in Biskupija is also founded on that of the churches of the medieval Croatian state.

There was a great flowering of art in the whole of Dalmatia, but particularly in the towns, in the Romanesque, Gothic and Renaissance periods. Dalmatian and foreign builders, painters, sculptors and stone masons left a wealth of works of art down the whole of the eastern Dalmatian coast. These make an unforgettable impression even on the ordinary observer, and an even deeper one on the artist. Meštrović himself mentioned the effect that old Dalmatian art had on his youthful mind when he was going away to study. Even in old age a journey that he had taken as a child with his father remained engraved on his memory for two things in particular — the sea and Šibenik cathedral. He also always remembered his childhood visits to Trogir and Split. The impression left on him by Radovan's wonderful Romanesque portal of Trogir Cathedral was even deeper than that made later in life by Rodin's

Gates of Hell. The same is true of the medieval carved wooden doors to Split cathedral, made by Buvina, which so much influenced his composition of the doors of the Otavice memorial and perhaps still more the frieze of wooden panels in the chapel of his *Kaštelet* in Split.

The great Croatian sculptor of the past with whom Meštrović had most in common was most certainly the late-Gothic sculptor and builder from Šibenik, Juraj the Dalmatian. The splendidly realized and realistically carved frieze of heads round Šibenik Cathedral, left an indelible impression on the boy. Juraj's *Scourging of Christ* in Split cathedral has not only formal likenesses to Meštrović's religious sculpture of later life, but its deep humanity and timelessness are echoed in similar themes by Meštrović such as his *Crucifixion* and *Lamentation*.

Meštrović was to repay his debt to Juraj the Dalmatian. One of his very last works was a monument to him in Šibenik.

Although during the period of the Turkish wars the full flowering of art in Dalmatia was halted, the national consciousness of the people was never quenched, and this led, in the second half of the nineteenth century, to a new artistic revival. Meštrović himself paid tribute to the pioneering work in Croatian and Yugoslav sculpture done by Ivan Rendić who conditioned the new urban classes to take art seriously and prepared the way for the generation of sculptors who followed him, especially Ivan Meštrović and Toma Rosandić. One of Meštrović's earliest works was a monument to the Split poet, Luka Botić, which had in fact been conceived by Ivan Rendić in openly Secessionist style, whereas Meštrović himself by then favoured a Rodinesque impressionism. Toma Rosandić took over the building of the memorial chapel of the Petrinović family in Supetar, which had been begun by Rendić.

The complex extent to which tradition and personal influence are intertwined may be illustrated by the following example. In 1900, as a young apprentice, Meštrović was engaged in the workshop of master mason Bilinić of Split, carving copies of human and animal figures for the medieval cathedral belfry which was at that time just being restored. Echoes of these console heads, animals and sphinxes can be traced in many of Meštrović's later works. In this Split workshop Meštrović received his first lessons in stone cutting from a slightly older sculptor, Toma Rosandić. Several years later Meštrović brought this same Rosandić to Vienna to carry out his sculptures in stone, and at the same time instructed him in sculptural modelling. Meštrović later became a master of stone carving, and Rosandić one of the most famous Yugoslav sculptors who later, as rector of the Academy of Art in Belgrade, taught several generations of young sculptors.

The formation and development of Meštrović's style is often explained as coming directly and exclusively from his contact with Vienna Secession, Rodin, Bourdelle, Assyrian and Greek sculpture and that of Michelangelo. In fact Meštrović was under very many influences in the shaping and enrichment of his artistic expression. One of the basic aspects of his art, in both the positive and negative sense, is the extent to which he was easily and richly influenced by the cultural heritage both of his own and other countries.

■

For the whole of his life Meštrović continually stressed those elements in his makeup which were expressly Slav, peasant and inland, or rather highland, although it is true that these did not reach fruition until they came into contact with the old Mediterranean and the contemporary European culture and art. He made a myth of his origins which especially appealed to the many literary people around him. The national, political, social and ideological situation at that time was particularly favourable for him. It was a period of the awakening and discovery of new, until then almost unknown, nations and of an urge to find in them something to refresh and revitalize contemporary European civilization and art which seemed surfeited and decadent.

But that Meštrović's insistence on his peasant origin was not a pose, or the result of fashionable demand, is shown by the fact that for the whole of his long life, and in spite of the wide culture that he acquired, he always felt himself to be a man of the people and was proud of his birth. As a child taking care of the goats and sheep in the mountains, he listened to and himself composed folk poems, and later, on all kinds of occasions, and even in old age in America, he was still able to recall this poetry and recited it with enthusiasm and emotion. In Vienna and Paris he exchanged the red peasant cap that he had started out into the world with for a broad brimmed artist's hat, but his face with its eagle nose, his broad sturdy way of moving, and his temperament always remained unchanged, that of a peasant from the stony Dalmatian Alps.

The discovery of such talent in a shepherd boy watching his sheep on Mount Svilaja, and decorating pieces of wood with his knife as a pastime, reminds us of a similar story of the painter Giotto. It was a parallel that became very popular, especially at the time of the swift ascent to fame of this new wonderchild just before the First World War. It is said that the Emperor Joseph himself, when he once met Meštrović walking in the grounds of Schönbrunn with his professor, asked him jokingly »How many sheep have you got?«

The sculptor's ancestor, also Ivan Meštrović but known as Aga, in face of the Turkish advance fled from Fojnica in Bosnia to Kossovo, near Drniš. He died in 1668, fighting against the Turks under Mount Livno. From that time onwards the family lived in the nearby village of Otavice. Meštrović's father, Mate Meštrović, whose nickname was Gabrilović, was a labourer and mason, he was known to have sometimes carved rustic stone decorations. His mother, Marta Kurabaš, figures in several of her son's well known sculptures as a woman of the people, with her firm, determined face.

His parents' poverty drove to work as hired labour in the grain-rich area of Slavonia. While they were retuning home after one such period of work Ivan Meštrović was born, August 15, 1883, in a stable in the Slavonian village of Vrpolje.

He did not go to school, but taught himself to read and write and thus made himself the only literate person in the village. Up to his fifteenth year he tended sheep on Mount Svilaja and listened to songs and tales about the heroes of the fight against the Turks. He learned to read by using the *Pjesmarica* (song-book) of Fra Andija Kačić a collection of folk literature. He also learned to read Vuk Karadžić's collection of national poems written in cyrillic. His uncle Joso noticed the boy's love of verse and brought him cheap editions of Kačić, of the great Montenegrin poet Njegoš, and of the modern Croatian poets Mažuranić and Vraz. He also liked to read the Bible. National poetry and Bible stories were his first sources of inspiration — and in the main remained his chief ones until his death.

Listening to and reading this folk poetry, and provoked by the example of the contemporary folk poet, Juraj Kapić, the boy began to write poetry himself on the same pattern. Some of these poems have survived and show the versatility of his youthful gifts.

The boy first became known for his carved decorations on distaffs. When he made a crutch for a wounded soldier he carved the lower part in the form of a shoe, and when this did not please changed it to a carving of a bare foot. He carved a Christ with open arms to ''embrace the whole world''. Then he turned his energies to modelling in plaster and clay and finally made his first experimental attempts to carve in stone. He made figures of peasant women, a cobbler, a Bosnian on a horse and then some of the famous figures of contemporary Croatian history, Ante Starčević and Bishop Strossmayer.

His unusual talent could not go unnoticed, not even in an almost invisible highland village. Many people later claimed to be responsible for his discovery, and in fact many were responsible, for the fame of the gifted shepherd boy very soon spread. First of all there was the local priest, Fra Marko Ćaćić, then the mayor of nearby Drniš, Nikola Adžija, and the archeologist of Croatian antiquities, Fra Luje Marun. In 1899, when he was only sixteen, the boy held an exhibition of his drawings in the tavern in Otavice, and under the figures of his heroes from national poetry he exhibited his own poems, composed in the ten-syllable folk style. This awakened the interest of the villagers to such an extent that they sent a parcel of his small sculptures to Jurje Biankini, editor of the Zadar paper *Narodni list*. He exhibited these works in the editorial office and printed the first account of the extraordinary talent of ''this labourer's son, Ivan Gabrilović Meštrović Martin, from the village of Otavice in the district of Drniš,'' asking if there was nobody who would pay for his schooling.

The villagers collected some money among themselves, and Adžija, at the beginning of 1900, took the boy, dressed in peasant costume, to Split. But the craft schools neither in Split nor in Zagreb would admit him as he had never been to school. Finally a place was found for him in the workshop of the Split master mason, Pavao Bilinić, who mainly made altars and grave memorials. He lived with a school teacher, Petar Škarica, who gave him instruction, and he attended evening courses for apprentices run by the Craft School and taught by Prof. Ante Bezić.

In Bilinić's workshop, near the railway station in Split harbour, young Meštrović learned how to carve simple stone decorations according to Gothic patterns. He was helped by a slightly older stone cutter, Toma Rosandić. More complex figures of saints for altars and gravestones were carved by an Italian sculptor Arturo Ferraroni. It was he who gave the boy his first lessons in figure modelling and carving.

Bilinić's wife Gina, daughter of the Split architect Vecchietti, and a drawing teacher, noticed the boy's exceptional intellegence and talent and began to give him drawing lessons.

Little by little everybody began to help him who had occasion to come into contact with his ability and capacity for hard work. One day he carved an angel himself, copied from another carving in the workshop, and in this way gained Bilinić's confidence. He was now allowed to carve in stone figures which others, mainly Ferraroni, modelled and marked on the stone. Very soon the news spread through Split that he could work better without ''a machine'' than the Italian could with, and another Split mason actually tried to entice Meštrović into his own workshop. After that Bilinić took him into his house, provided him with board and lodging and paid him for his work.

While still an apprentice Meštrović came to know the elderly Croatian sculptor Ivan Rendić, who was in Split at that time making a statue of the mayor, Gajo Bulat. It is said that he actually worked in Rendić's studio, which is difficult to believe, but even if he had Rendić could hardly have had any great influence on him in so short a time, except perhaps to encourage him to get himself trained.

After ten months work in Bilinić's workshop it was made possible for the boy to get proper schooling. The whole town was already talking about him, and a retired officer, called Grubišić, managed to interest Alexander König in him. König was a Viennese industrialist and the owner of mines in Dalmatia. He sent Meštrović to Vienna.

Meštrović arrived in the huge, bustling European city dressed in peasant costume and with his round red peasant cap on his head. He did not know a word of German and, unfortunately for him, König lost all further interest in him. But Meštrović would not return. He had decided that he would somehow manage to stay until he got a training. Luckily for him he found lodgings with a hospitable Czech called Sycora who taught him German.

But the Art Academy would not allow him to study there because he had no previous schooling. He had to find someone who would prepare him for the entrance exam. Professor Bitterlich, a teacher at the Academy, would not show any personal interest in the boy, and demanded 400 crowns to prepare him. This Meštrović did not have. All he then received was a little help from Drniš district. Sycora introduced him to Otto König, a retired professor of sculpture of the Vienna Applied Arts School, who agreed to prepare him for the entrance exam free. Sycora's interest in the boy was so great that he actually put a room in his house at his disposal so that he could work at home, and ordered a barrel of clay for him.

Otto König (1838—1920) was unable to help the boy in any but the technical sense, for he was not well known as a sculptor, and mainly made figures according to trade orders. Meštrović worked in his studio for seven months. First of all he copied one of König's own figures and some rococo heads, and then did a lifesize portrait of König himself. This portrait, a copy of one of Michelangelo's early *Pieta* and a number of free carvings were taken by König to show Edmund Hellmer, Director of the Academy of Art. Hellmer recognized the boy's gifts and agreed to take him if he could pass the entrance exam in spite of opposition from other professors.

Meštrović spent four years at the Academy and passed all his exams regularly. He soon had to leave Sycora who himself was in difficulties at the time. This period was the most difficult of the boy's whole life. He had the tiny sun of 12 florins monthly, sent by the Zagreb Artists' Association. He lived with a worker's family and ate in a canteen. For two years he suffered real hunger and misery although he did get help from a student organization in Vienna. After this things improved a little and the Dalmatian District Assembly awarded him a monthly sum of 30 florins. With this he had to live and to pay for his studio, materials and models.

Meštrović studied at the Academy industriously, but it could not contribute anything much to the formation of his artistic personality. For this he had to work, read and find his models outside the cold academic regime.

His first teacher was Edmund Hellmer (1850—1919) who had to his credit a large number of public statues done in a compromise style somewhere between classical and baroque, for example those of Goethe, Mozart and Johan Strauss. Later he studied under Hans Bitterlich (b. 1860) who had made the monument to Gutenberg and Queen Elizabeth in Vienna. He did not have any influence on his pupil either. Two teachers of architecture were much more important, Ohmann and Wagner. Frederich Ohmann (1858—1927) was the chief architect of the Vienna Court, professor in Vienna and Prague and had made a considerable number of monuments and buildings in which he strove to fuse classical style with modern tendencies. He was the author of the project for the Archeological Museum in Split. Otto Wagner was one of the most outstanding personalities in Vienna at that time, one of the most famous teachers at the Academy and the most outstanding figure in Austrian and indeed in European architecture. He was against academic eclecticism and (1899—1905) was the leader of the Vienna Secession movement, although in fact he disowned many of their ideas later on. In his work he paid equal attention to architecture, interior decoration, furniture and all other details. He had a great effect on many famous architects and in Yugoslavia especially on J. Plečnik and V. Kovačić. In the field of architecture his effect on Meštrović was decisive. Many of Wagner's ideas, which are those of Secession, were taken over by Meštrović in his plans for his early architectural work, especially in the greatest of them all, the never realized *Vidovdan Temple*. It was Wagner who awoke in Meštrović an interest in architecture, and a synthesis between building and sculpture.

From the year 1903 onwards Meštrović regularly showed his work in the exhibitions of the Vienna Secession Group, and was accepted as a member of their Selection Committee.

Secession was not however the most basic influence on his style even then but rather its complete opposite, French impressionism. The effect of impressionism would not have been of such great importance if it had not been for the personality of the great French sculptor Rodin.

We must explain here the apparent contradiction that Meštrović when in Vienna worked in the style of French impressionism and when in Paris in that of Vienna Secession, although one might expect the contrary. Meštrović did not go to Paris until 1904, after finishing his studies in the Academy. But his acquaintance with Rodin and Rodin's work was of earlier date. He knew him from Vienna although he had never been his pupil.

August Rodin (1840—1917) came to fame in the Paris International Exhibition of 1900. His vital figures, with their powerful movement, and play of light and shadow were the exact opposite of the cold classicism of that time and the opposite too of much academic realism. After the Paris exhibition Rodin travelled with his sculptures to most of the main European cities, among them Vienna. Official academic circles rejected the French sculptor, considering him, like Meunier, "too revolutionary". But the younger artists, regardless of the reigning Secession movement, acknowledged his greatness, and when he visited Vienna in 1902 he was enthusiastically received by them. It was then that young Meštrović made Rodin's acquaintance.

Not until much later did Meštrović come to know Rodin better and even come to be friendly with him. In 1907 he had an exhibition in Paris. Rodin, by then an old man, became interested in the exhibition and invited the young sculptor to come and visit him in Meudon. Two or three years later Meštrović once again visited Rodin in Paris, but their acquaintance did not ripen into friendship until the years of the First World War when they were both in Rome. Rodin often visited Meštrović's studio in Rome, and it was here that Meštrović made a portrait of him. They remained close friends until Rodin's death in 1917.

Rodin had the highest opinion of Meštrović's work, although in later years it was the opposite of his own. His pronouncement that Meštrović was the greatest phenomenon among sculptors is well known, and when Prince George Karadjordjević asked the old sculptor, also a friend of his, who would take his place Rodin replied "Don't worry, your Meštrović is greater than I am". Rodin confessed to Meštrović that he had begun working in stone too late, that sculpture was primarily expression in stone. He also told him that he had discovered the importance of architecture too late.

Rodin's influence on Young Meštrović was immediate and powerful, although it could not satisfy him in the ideological sense. Indeed there were few in that period of cold academic classicism or genteel naturalistic sculpture who could withstand Rodin's genius. Antoine Bourdelle, like Meštrović' fundamentally a sculptor with goals very different from Rodin's said of his teacher: "Yes, we were all of us influenced by him, we copied his way of working: whatever he did there was an inescapable attraction, a light shone out from his works which lit the whole field of art". Meštrović spoke of the anguish that Rodin's death gave him because of the spiritual ties that had been between them and because for him it was the loss of the second great spirit (the first had been Tolstoy) that had had a profound effect on him and contributed to his own formation.

Two works in particular stand out in this impressionistic phase of Meštrović's work: the monument of *Luka Botić* in Split (1905) and *The Well of Life* in front of the theatre in Zagreb (1905). In particular the first variant the *Bust of Botić* (Split Art Gallery) has a marked harmony and unity of composition, a sensitiveness in the restless surface treatement and a great feeling for space and volume. This statue lacks, what in fact most of Rodin's statues also lack, monumentality.

The *Well of Life* which stands in front of the National Theatre in Zagreb, is another work of maturity and artistic quality. The influence of Rodin is obvious both in the technique and also in the preoccupation with a philosophical problem of general human significance (as in *The Gates of Hell, Eternal Spring, The Kiss, Kneeling Man, Eternal Idol* etc.). In *The Well of Life* Meštrović achieved a happy synthesis of sculpture and reflective symbolism. The well shape gives extra meaning to the circle of figures bound by the common idea of ''everlasting thirst'', the figures are thus more than a decorative frieze. One might in fact say that the young Meštrović, although superficially using an impressionistic technique and creating each figure separately, almost naturalistically, achieved a certain unity of expression which Rodin in his *Gates of Hell* was not wholly able to achieve.

In the period 1900—1904, while under the spell of impressionism Meštrović, working in Vienna, made 25 sculptures: portraits, nudes, figural compositions, etc.

When we consider the entire work of Meštrović we see that, after all, Rodin's impressionism played a less important part than some other elements. It is true that for the first whole decade of this century he could not rid himself of some elements of impressionism, and also that at the end of his life, in America, he came back to it at least partly. Nevertheless it was far from his basic feeling which was for size and stylization, for stressing sculpture in the round rather than the vibrating interplay of light and shadow.

The impact of Secession, especially Vienna Secession, was far more important especially in the short but intensively creative period when Meštrović was making his *Kossovo Cycle*. Why was it then that when young he did not immediately take to Secession as a progressive and revolutionary style? When the *avant-garde* Viennese artists of 1897 rallied behind Secession there was an anarchic element in their programme. They were out to destroy the set bourgeois and academic tradition, to destroy even the whole cultural inheritance. Young Meštrović, until lately a shepherd, with even his elementary schooling incomplete, could hardly be satiated and revolted by bourgeois culture. He had only just come in contact with it. The masterpieces of classical and medieval art in the museums of Vienna and the plaster casts of the Academy were a real discovery and experience for him. In fact Secession was a reaction against the momentary and picturesque effects of impressionism, mainly in painting it is true, but in sculpture also. It was a search for something more lasting, symbolic and monumental, all the things that impressionism did not offer. The young Meštrović was so inspired by Rodin's creative genius that he took his style from him as well. Rodin was the end of a rich period of art history and Meštrović at that time, like the Janus of old, had one face turned towards the past and the other towards the future, trying to unite the two in his work.

Although the Secession movement used many elements from the cultural past it was essentially a revolutionary and progressive ideology. Scholastic eclecticism and a continual turning over of the pages of the picture books of past ages gave way to free creation, with a special feeling for the decorative. When in Paris Meštrović spent whole days amoung the museum collections of the Louvre. It was not just Pheidias's works that attracted him, but even more the secrets of the monumental sculptures of the ancient cultures of Assyria, Babylon and Egypt, and the Mediterranean sculpture of the pre-classical and classical culture of Greece.

The ideas and style of the Vienna Secession were decisive for Meštrović's further work. He came to accept them in the last years of his work in Vienna, but he did not fully apply them until he was working in Paris 1907—1909, and then used them right down to 1914.

In 1897 about 20 young Viennese artists broke away from the Society of Art and founded their own breakaway group called *Sezession* or *Vereinigung bildender Künstler Oesterreichs*. The leaders of this group were the painters Rudolf von Alt and Gustav Klimt, and their periodical was called *Ver sacrum*. More artists soon joined and two other periodicals spread their ideas and at the same printed detailed and complimentary accounts of the work of Meštrović. These were Munich *Die Kunst* and the Darmstadt *Deutsche Kunst und Dekoration*. The main characteristics of Secession were: personal freedom, emancipation from the past, variety, and especially an attempt to find a synthesis of architecture, sculpture, painting and applied arts and crafts.

A French current that had similarities with the Secession movement in Vienna, Munich and Berlin was the Paris *art nouveau,* and some decorative and neoimpressionist elements in the paintings of Gaugin, Puvis de Chavanne, and Toulouse Lautrec. Even Rodin and Meunier exhibited in the Secession exhibitions although they had no real ties with the movement.

The German, Austrian and Swiss painters Hans von Marees, Max Liebermann, Ferdinand Hodler, Franz von Stuck, Wilhelm Trübner, Lovis Corinth and the romantic Arnold Böcklin were much nearer Secession, and so were the periodicals *Brücke* and *Blaue Reiter*.

It was not sculptors that had the greatest impact on Meštrović in so far as this style is concerned, for among them there were no forceful personalities, rather he was influenced by architects and painters. The greatest sculptural works were Max Klinger's statue of Beethoven and Franz Metzner's (1870—1919) *Volkerschlachtdenkmal* (Struggle of the Nations). These, and especially the second which depicts national struggle, have some connection with Meštrović's style, but the effect that it had on his *Vidovdan Temple* is often much overrated.

Franz Metzner was also self-taught. He taught sculpture at the Vienna School of Applied Art 1903—1906, at the time that Meštrović was studying in Vienna. He too for a time, for example when he did the *Nibelungen Well* in Vienna, was much under the influence of Rodin and then turned towards symbolism and stylization. But he had none of Meštrović's power, fertility and splendid talent and what influence there was was reciprocal. This is the more so since Meštrović carved his statues for the *Vidovdan Temple* all at one time in Paris 1907—1909 while Schmitz and Metzner worked on their *Struggle of the Nations* from 1906 to 1913.

Meštrović did not have a very high opinion of Metzner's sculpture and considered him more a ceramist than a sculptor.

Among other outstanding sculptors working in the same vein mention may be made of the Czech, Hugo Lederer (1871—1940), the link between him and Meštrović being their common admiration for Michelangelo, also Jan Šturs (1880—1925). He was the teacher of another Croatian sculptor, Kršinić, and his nudes have something in common with Meštrović's nudes. The German sculptor Adolf E. R. Hildebrand (1847—1921) also had a considerable influence at this time. He was an old man, fed up with neo-baroque decoration, and enthusiastic about the purity of Roman sculpture. In all his work his main stress is on simplicity and monumentality and the harmonization of sculpture and architecture. It was his work and his theories published in *Problems of Form* that began Meštrović's disenchantment with Rodin's impressionism.

The architects of the Secession group had a great influence on Meštrović, particularly the strongest personality among them, his own teacher, Otto Wagner (1841—1918). He it was who developed a feeling for architecture in Meštrović and encouraged his ambitions in this field. He paid equal attention to every detail of a building from outward appearance down to the work of each individual craftsman. When Meštrović was in Vienna Wagner was the leading spirit of the Secessionist stream (1900—1905). His production and activities especially in the Technological Museum, the New Academy of Art and the University Library in Vienna, and the works of his best pupils such as the architects Joseph Olbrich and Joseph Hoffman had a decisive influence on a whole generation. Even the builder of the Leipzig *Memorial to the Struggle of the Nations*, Metzner's collaborater Bruno Schmitz, was Wagner's pupil.

Between 1901—1907 Meštrović made 50 different works in Vienna and about 20 during the summer holidays in Split, where his one-time master, Bilinić, put his workshop at his disposal and Toma Rosandić helped him in the stone carving.

At this time Meštrović was exhibiting new works in Vienna almost every year. He exhibited his *Mother and Child* when only a second year student. Its blatant naturalism scandalized the conservative public and Meštrović found himself in conflict with the organizers of the exhibition. As a result the Secession Group invited him to exhibit in future in their annual Shows. The following year he was made a member of their society, and only a little later given the honour of being on their Selection Committee. He showed regularly with them from 1903 to 1910. In 1904 he and another Croatian sculptor and friend, Tomislav Križman, exhibited together in their studio on the top of a building in Beatrix Gasse, high over the roofs of Vienna. This first exhibition of his collected works gained him some recognition and follwers, among them the big Viennese industrialist Wittgenstein, who from this time onwards frequently ordered work from Meštrović. The third member of the Croatian art colony then in Vienna was Mirko Rački. With these two Meštrović was more than just friendly, they shared the same views about art and patriotism. It was at this time that he met and married Ruža Klein, who lived in Vienna but was Croatian by birth. She was a painter herself, very greatly contributed to his general education and opened up to him many circles in Vienna. He supported himself by commissioned works, what he sold at his exhibitions, and copies made of the old masters in the Imperial Museum.

Meštrović exhibited at other collective exhibitions besides that of the Secession Group, for example at the First Yugoslav Art Exhibition in Belgrade 1904, at the Hagebund exhibition in Vienna 1904, at the jubilee exhibition of the Artists' Society in Zagreb 1905, at the International Exhibition in London 1906, at the Second Exhibition of the Society of Yugoslav Artists, Lada, in Sofia, at the exhibition of the Croatian Art Society in Zagreb 1906, with the Yugoslav Colony in Belgrade 1907, at the Venice Art Exhibition 1907 etc. All these exhibitions added to his reputation, but he did not achieve real fame until he had made and exhibited his sculpture for the *Kossovo Cycle*. Only in 1910 did he come to the attention of critics on a European level, before that it was largely his own countrymen who had been enthusiastic about him, first Filip Marušič, then Milan Begović, Božo Lovrić, Josip Kosor, Branimir Livadić, Antun Gustav Matoš almost all of them the best representatives of Croatian literature at that time. It is perhaps interesting to note that as early as 1905 the Croatian critic and artist Izidor Kršnjavi, not in general well disposed towards new movements, wrote in his "Survey of the Development of Croatian Art" that among young artists Ivan Meštrović had a leading place.

The aims that Meštrović had set himself were of the highest. Not only was he not content to be noticed only in his own small country where, as he somewhere said, "even a little tree stands out if there is no forest", he was not even satisfied that he should be compared with his own contemporaries for all of them, and he himself, seemed small in comparison to the great masters of the past.

After Karl Wittgenstein had bought his second well *At the Source of Life* and several other works, he went on a two months trip to Italy and Paris. It was then that he first came in contact with the work of Michelangelo who was to be the constant companion of his imaginative life from then on. He also got to know the works of the contemporary French sculptors Bourdelle and Maillol. In 1907 Meštrović moved to Paris although he still retained his studio in Valleriestrasse and continued to exhibit with the Secession Group. In Paris he rented a studio in Impasse de Maine and went to work almost like a maniac, breaking his tempo only to visit museums and galleries.

Already in 1908 he showed ten sculptures in Paris in the Salon d'Automne and five in Salon National des Artistes Français. These exhibitions caught the attention of the Paris public and it was after a visit to one of them that Rodin invited Meštrović to come and see him so that he could personally congratulate him. In 1909 he actually exhibited 18 works in the Salon d Automne, and had the honour of being elected to be a member of the committee of the salon.

Meštrović at this time was so obsessed with the figures of his *Kossovo Cycle* that he had no time to move among the art circles of Paris. We know only that he met Rodin and Bourdelle. Just before his own death, when he revisited his homeland, he stayed for a few days in Paris to see once more the scenes of the happiest days of his youth. He visited the Louvre, the classical sculptures of Venus de Milo, and Hero. He also went to Rodin's house and museum where he had spent so many days and nights talking with the old sculptor and Bourdelle and finally visited Bourdelle's widow in Montmartre.

What had Paris to offer that could have a further shaping effect on Meštrović's style? Not a great deal. For Rodin had already had his quickening influence Meštrović had come from Vienna full to the brim with Secession, and though this had still not come to full expression in his work, it was in this style that he was able to give the fullest and most complete form to the ideas he then had. Style and ideas were like some great force ready to combine and surge forth carrying him forward. Nevertheless there were the underground halls of the Louvre, and there were Bourdelle and Maillol.

It would be a mistake to look for the prototypes of the puzzling sphinxes and stylized heroes of the *Vidovdan Temple* in the Assyrian and Babylonian sculpture of the Louvre. But inspiration there certainly was for him, hidden in the dim arcaded halls, crammed with reliefs, sculptures and decorative elements from buildings. This was something quite different from the lyric excitement of Rodin's sculpture. Here Meštrović found himself faced with something secret and hidden in mysterious stone masses, something which needed long study before meaning could be puzzled out. But gradually he found they had more to offer than the works of the impressionists, and they always seemed to promise something new, something that could not be completely discovered or understood. The stone revealed its secrets in the special language of a material in which the centuries seemed to be compressed, with all their wars and religions, their times of flowering and of cataclysm.

Then too these halls revealed to him pre-classical Greek sculpture which had previously been neglected and despised in comparison with the sculpture of the golden age of Pheidras, Myron and Praxiteles. And in these reticent and monolithic shapes, in these enigmatic faces, with their inscrutable smiles, in the decorative rhythm of the clothing, the hair and manes bringing to mind the Aegian waves of times long gone by, the young Meštrović discovered history and myth, love and hate, victimization and revenge and hope in the future. It is true that there was much here that had the flavour of literary ideas, the philosophy was not very deep, but from this Egyptian, Assyrian, Babylonian and ancient Greek sculpture he learned something that whole generations of nineteenth century sculptors had not learned: to value stone as the basic, the noblest and best material for sculpture; stone and work in stone. He learned to value to the full what could be achieved with the chisel, the graver and the mallet. Even when modelling was done in clay or when casts were made in plaster, he always had stone before his eyes as the final material.

Emile-Antoine Bourdelle (1861—1929) had an elemental and temperamental nature like Meštrović's. He was almost twenty years older and had a great influence on him. He too was at first enthusiastic about Rodin and he too later had a reaction similar to that of Meštrović.

"As soon as I was able to measure the curve of his genius, I ceased to consider myself his pupil," he said. His sculpture is architectually composed and basically monumental. He did not, as Rodin did, force his material, he used it to present a vision of life and did all he could to make his figures seem to have a life of their own. This was something that Meštrović was able to learn from him. He learned far more than from the essentially eclectic Hildebrand or the superficial Metzner.

"To model means to destroy," said Bourdelle, "to build means to create." Bourdelle, the architectural sculptor, defeated Rodin, the analytic sculptor, in Meštrović. It is not unimportant that Bourdelle too was from the village and imbued his works with an elemental vehemence and roughness.

But there was a difference between Bourdelle and Meštrović nevertheless. Behind the first stood whole centuries of culture, culture on the wane, and behind Meštrović only primaeval legend and before him a future that was just dawning. A little later the Italian writer and critic Ugo Ojetti, and the sculptor Leonardo Bistolfi entered into fruitless discussion as to whether Meštrović influenced Bourdelle or the other way round.

Luckily however at that time Meštrović had not completely ceased to use Rodin's manner of modelling, and only later was he to take over Bourdell's "cutting" technique.

The work of the third great French sculptor of this time, Aristid Maillol (1861—1944) also influenced Meštrović. Although Maillol continued in the tradition of Renoir and Rodin experiencing form as natural volume, he freed it from the restless impressionist treatment of surface, the interplay of concave and convex surfaces, of light and shadow.

In these stormy years in his Paris studio young Meštrović grappled with the problems of his art. He worked in clay and created with a wide freedom the first basic forms and contours, as Bourdelle would have done. Then with the pleasure of Maillol he forced these masses of material to yield huge human figures, but without neglecting the analytical treatment of individual parts. There was neither money nor time to create directly in stone, nevertheless Meštrović, modelling in clay, always kept before him the final idea of stone. Hard, monumental stone represented to his imagination something special, something in his own personal and national tradition and at the some time his future. And so, although many of the sculptures of this period did show restless movement, like *Miloš Obelić* (1908; Belgrade) and the relief *Dancers* (1913; Split), it is no longer intimate Rodinesque restlessness, it is movement and turbulence on a wide scale and within firmly controlled masses.

Nationalist ideology and Secession decoration are of only superficial importance in the splendid nudes of the widows of Kossovo. The basic reality is that of the Southern temperament. The pure joy in a woman's body and in white stone suggest something of the breath of Maillol's sculpture. When we look at *Psyche, Memoires* or *At Rest* we forget that at first they were to bear the names of the widows of Kossovo Field, especially when we look at them under the blue sky of Meštrović's villa in Split. They cannot help but recall Maillol's poetic and at the same time monumental figures in marble, *Méditerrané* for example.

But all these were only surface influences on Meštrović. He never became the follower of any one teacher, never gave himself up completely to any single stream or influence. In his Paris studio ideas came to him one after another. The conception of his *Kossovo (Vidovdan) Temple* developed with lightning speed, the figures took on huge proportions, and this demanded from him faster and faster work which often exceeded his physical and mental capabilities. According to Herbert Read "every art form is the expression of will, the satisfaction of some desire" — and Meštrović's style was an expression of his psychological longings.

He already had the idea of the *Kossovo Temple* when he was in Vienna. He made the first sketches for it in 1905 and 1906, but most of the figures were made in Paris in 1907, 1908 and right down to 1910, the year he first exhibited them at the Vienna Secession Exhibition. Basic to his idea was the centuries long desire for freedom and unity among the South Slavs. The final impulse to this was given by the Austro-Hungarian annexation of Bosnia and Hercegovina, which seemed the last phase of the tragedy of the South Slavs that began with the Turkish occupation.

Meštrović himself many times, in explaining how he came to have the idea for his never to be finished *Kossovo* or *Vidovdan Temple* said:

What I had in mind was an attempt to create a synthesis of popular national ideals and their development, to express in stone and building how deeply buried in each one of us are the memories of the great and decisive moments of our history — I wanted at the same time to create a focus of hope in the future standing out in the countryside and under the free sky.

It was after the Turkish invasion and the defeat of the Serbs on Kossovo Field, on St. Vid s (St. Vitus') Day, 1389 that the Serbs lost their freedom and later all the South Slavs. But the desire for freedom through centuries burned on as a live force in the subject nations. The slain heroes of Kossovo became the heroes of national poetry, and were used to inspire the people in a continual struggle against the Turks. It was a folk legend that the greatest hero of all, Kraljević Marko, was not dead but only slept and that he would wake when freedom was achieved. This folk legend for centuries kept alive in the South Slavs the hope of liberty. It was an ideal that was bigger than boundaries of nationality and faith and shone as a common light for all oppressed people from the Soča to the Bojana.

Thus Meštrović in his *Kossovo Temple* wished to create a religion of martyrdom and of hope.

He was not the only creative artist whose work was inspired by the tragedy of the Turkish conquest. Before him there had been the Renaissance poet Marko Marulić who wrote *Judith*, Ivan Gundulić's *Osman*, Andrija Kačić's *Pleasant Talks of the Slav Nations*, Peter Njegoš's *Highland Wreath,* and more recently Ivan Mažuranić's *The Death of Smail Aga Čengić* and Ivo Vojnović's *Death of the Mother of the Jugovići*. In all these the same idea prevailed; tragedy, slavery and hope of freedom.

The Turks it is true had gone, but other occupying powers were still there and the people were not free. The Austrians, Hungarians and Italians treated the lands of the South Slavs as if they were colonies, and Meštrović in the Kossovo tragedy wished to create something that would be a symbol of all the suffering and all the hopes for freedom and unity of all South Slavs.

Impelled by an idea of such width and involvement, in which the *Kossovo Temple* was supposed to be a focus of unity for so many nations and religions, so much suffering and hope, it is understandable that for him it came to represent a whole confused complex of ideas, symbols, mysticism and emotion.

Meštrović wrapped himself in a cloud of symbolism which found most adequate expression in the Vienna Secession style. But in his declamatory and emotional approach he was supported by someone else. Meštrović himself was too close to the village and to reality for him, left to himself, to have veered so far away from real life. The someone else was his older and admired friend, the poet Ivo Vojnović. The denunciatory tone of Vojnović's drama about the bereaved mother of the seven Jugovići killed on Kossovo field, *The Death of the Mother of the Jugovići*, was throwing the Croatian and Serbian youth of that time into ecstacies bordering on delirium. It was something between *fin de siecle* literature, religion, patriotism and politics. In his sculpture for the *Kossovo Cycle* Meštrović very quickly adapted himself to Vojnović's style, and Vojnović in his turn became a theatrical interpreter of Meštrović's sculptures.

We have direct evidence of the beginnings of this Promethian inspiration. While a student in Vienna Meštrović every summer spent a few months in Split where there was a very active group of intellectuals, artists and bohemians, at the same time he would visit his parents in the village. One summer night in an attic room on *Narodni trg* there was a meeting of Meštrović with the painter Vidović, the composer Hatze and the poet Vojnović who declaimed with great emotion his lines on the mother of the Jugovići and the tragedy of Kossovo. This drama had by then become, especially for the Dalmatian youth, a symbol of the struggle for freedom and South Slav unity. It moved Meštrović to great excitement and sowed in him the seed of his *Kossovo Temple*. A fertile field for this seed to grow in was provided by the Secession style which just at that moment Meštrović had really begun to take to, as part of his emergence from impressionism.

To try and describe all the ideas and symbolism of this Temple would take us too far. So much was said and written about it just before, during and immediately after the First World War that it has ceased to be art and become religion or even empty verbiage. This verbiage, by people who used Meštrović's patriotic feelings but were incapable of understanding his art, has also provoked socially motivated critics. The artistic qualities of the work are obscured in a thick forest of other considerations.

This is how Meštrović's friend, the writer A. Tresić Pavičić, wrote about the meaning of the *Vidovdan Temple:*

This temple carries a weight of symbolism in every detail. The foundations represent the countless Serbian and Croatian victims, who lost their lives in five centuries of struggle for the glory of the Cross and for golden freedom; the great columns symbolize the leading heroes and statesmen, the suffering to attain freedom of those upon whom the burden of our homeland rests; the water font symbolises the tears and blood that have been shed; the belfry the pure souls of the heroes flying to heaven, a link between heaven and earth; the bells are heralds of victory over evil, of the peace of God among all peoples.

For a number of years Meštrović worked on a huge wooden model of his *Kossovo Temple* and this aroused great interest and even sensation at various exhibitions. The building and sculpture were compared to Constantine Meunier's *Monument to Work,* to Rodin's monument of which only The *Gates of Hell* were finished, and with that other projected monument of Rodin's The *Belfry of Work,* with Metzner's memorial The *Struggle of the Nations* and even with the least successful of all these similar attempts the monument to the *Fallen Warriors* in Rome. But these were all later associations. If any building was used by Meštrović as a pattern it was the Roman and medieval group of buildings forming the Peristyle, the Mausoleum and the belfry of Split Cathedral.

Entrance to a peristyle was to be through a monumental gate, similar to the triumphal arches of old. Then was to come a central building with a cupola and an ambulatory around it, just like Diocletian's mausoleum. In front was to be a belfry, exactly like the Romanesque belfry of Split cathedral, only in place of columns were to be the figures of the heroes of Kossovo. Under the cupola in the centre of the building was to stand the huge equestrian statue of *Kraljević Marko*. Right and left were to be two small domed chapels. If we then add the sphinx, also inspired by that in Diocletian's Palace, then we truly do not need to look farther for the architectural pattern of the *Kossovo Temple* than Split. Of course the stylistic impact of Secession and especially of Wagner played their part.

Meštrović was fully aware of the enormous efforts that would be needed for the building of such a temple with hundreds of stone carved figures. Part of his vision was that it should be built over several generations by collective efforts, just as the medieval cathedrals were. The state would provide the materials and all those working on the temple, artists and craftsmen alike, would get the same pay, enough to let them live normally. Sculptors, architects and master-craftsmen would at the same time teach the younger generations and thus the building site would be at one and the same time a vast centre of learning, and keep up the old and noble tradition of building, masonry, and sculpture.

But when the Serbs, Croats and Slovenes gained their freedom the main motive force for the building of the temple disappeared. The liberators, who very soon became a ruling class, wanted to raise monuments to themselves, not to heroes of the past and so the temple was never realized. Some of Meštrović's sculptures were carried out in stone, some remained in plaster and some got lost or broken or, like the central colossus *Kraljević Marko*, they were scattered all over the place. Nothing was left but the memory of a great idea and superhuman effort, and many individual sculptures which have made Yugoslav and foreign galleries the richer.

Let us return to Meštrović's gallery in Paris in 1907 when he was still grappling with his great ideas and when he was trying to make use of all the experience he had acquired until then in Vienna and in Paris, to use to the full all his talent and technical mastery.

It was Bourdelle's principles of architectural sculpture that he was working by, and which Bourdelle himself was not so fully able to realize in practice as Meštrović in this period:

The time has come to build! We need once more to rediscover the principles of monumentality, once more to find a link between the constructional values of statues and their sculptural quality; we must master composition and mass, our creation must be on a vast level, we must balance detail and whole. Finally we must become the masters of the technique we use, patiently working under the guidance of the whole heart, the whole mind and the whole spirit.

A large number of Meštrović's great works date from this period. It was a time when he executed almost 50 sculptures almost all of them more than lifesize. It is difficult to imagine even the pure physical effort that this must have cost. His aim was daring and unattainable: the building of the *Vidovdan Temple* composed of hundreds of huge sculptures, telamons, caryatids, sphinxes, heroes and widows, something big enough to be an almost mystical assertion of the sufferings of his people. The conception was doomed to failure in advance like Rodin's *Gates of Hell*. There were two fatal contradictions in it from the very first: that one man could not possibly finish it, and that Meštrović considered the sculpture as an essential element in the building which was to the detriment of both.

At that time, and to a lesser extent even later, Meštrović conceived architecture as a monumental collection of sculptures the whole given unity by serving a single idea. This was behind his *Vidovdan Temple* and behind his later sculptural buildings, *Avala* and the memorial chapel in Cavtat. He made the fatal and basic mistake in that, unlike Bourdelle and Maillol, Brancusi and Moore, he was not conscious of the architectural structure as such (although in some cases his natural talent allowed him to realize it subconsciously). He conceived of architectural forms primarily as in sculpture, as a matter of volume not space.

The figures which he did for his temple were part of the imagined architectural whole. It is only because his great natural talent broke through that when he was carving Banović Strahinja he created what is now known as *Torso* (1907; London), and in creating the widow Vukosava he made the statue *Memories* (1907; Belgrade). And what about all the other numberless human figures, and sphinxes that never came to the stage of being independent sculptures? Of them only fragments of a great but basically unattainable idea remain. How much Meštrović could have created in this enormously fertile period if he had been more economical with his genius, if he had concentrated on individual objects! How much greater would have been his contribution to world art had he not been obsessed with the patriarchal and mystical creation of the warriors and the widows of Kossovo, if he had confined himself to human figures!

His inspiration and at the same time his handicap was his national ideology. Although working in Paris he kept himself apart from the "decadent" West. His studio was in fact to him a little free portion of an unfree homeland. This fixed preoccupation with his country's problems, this fixed looking backwards to Kossovo, to the world of Mount Svilaja, this enormous emotional relationship towards rawhide sandals, the round red peasant cap, the monotonous rhythm of folk poetry and the peasant fiddle are the springs of Meštrović's early conservatism while he worked at the fount of modern art. It is an echo of retarded national romanticism.

Meštrović himself later admitted this:

I could not escape the fate of my own origins, and all that they mean in the narrow, in the broad and in the broadest sense.

The results were very complex, good and bad. They left an indelible mark on me and on all that I created.

It would however be quite wrong to consider the role that patriotism played in Meštrović's work, either then or later, as a fetter. Meštrović almost never made a figure for its own sake. The desire to create was in him always awoken and shaped by ideas. At first these ideas were of a general humanistic and metaphysical nature, later patriotic, national, religious and then again, at the end of his life humanistic and metaphysical. We must remember that in those years Ivan Meštrović was active in politics and in public life, he was the centre and one of the leading personalities of the Yugoslav nationalists, and an active member of the Yugoslav Committee. If we forget this it is difficult to understand how he was able to use his artistic and aesthetic feelings in the service of national and political goals. But as he himself said:

"...Those difficult war years, and the position of we Yugoslavs... made it impossible for us not to use the tones and style of propaganda. For me, and for all of us, the most important consideration of all was our national fate, it was more pressing even than art — if indeed one can imagine art without a goal, an idea:"

We must not forget that from childhood he had had an obvious affinity for literature, and the literature to which he had been exposed was the strongly emotional literature of national poetry and Biblical psalms. When still a child he wrote folk poetry, then essays, compositions for special occasions, personal notes and observations, reflective and religious passages etc. This literary side of Meštrović had a very important effect on his creative side, and it was more often a negative than a positive one. But without it his sculptures would not have been his. And although his *Widow* or *Memories* are no longer thought of as part of the Kossovo tragedy, as he perhaps would have wished, they are certainly more profound works of art because of their underlying feeling of suffering and sorrow. And although in *Kraljević Marko* and *Miloš Obilić* we need not read the story of the struggle of the Serbs against the Turks, we feel in them a note of human rebellion and revolt. Meštrović could never be content with only artistic and aesthetic ideas, he could not create at all unless fired by feelings of broader significance. "My life will have proved to have meaning if my conception of the *Vidovdan Temple* and my artistic work as a whole are an expression of the unification of Yugoslavia," he said in 1915.

His romantic and mystical ideology often had a direct effect on his style. Obviously in his "heroic" style we should not try to find any essentially Slav or national characteristics, as his own contemporaries, and even more so the generation after him, did. It is true that to a certain extent he forced his style in order to make it express his philosophical and didactic ideas, and this meant that in both style and spirit he was behind world art of his time, in some cases it was actually a case of conscious conservative retroaction. To the Italian sculptor Bistolfije in 1914 he said:

"I, like my people, until now considered to be barbarians or some kind of lower race, feel a lack of certainty in European culture, and that is why we express ourselves in a manner that is not in keeping with the way of thinking and the way of expressing thoughts that is common in Europe. But I know that what my people feel can be beautiful and human, and so can the way they try to express it."

Because his ideas were so often vague and utopistic, (Tolstoy was a more important master to him than Rodin), Meštrović was not able to understand contemporary art. He said himself: "I have never either hated the times in which I live nor underestimated them, but

I have tried not to overestimate them either, not to separate them from times gone by but, as far as I can, to see them as a preparation for future times, always fostering enthusiasm for times to come, which needs must be better than times gone by."

As a result of this attitude his aspirations were too great to be realized. There is much that is tragic in his later acceptance of this. Writing of his work up to 1933 he said it was almost all: "nothing more than notes, sketches and studies, preparations for all that which I wanted to say more completely and fully. For that reason I feel that my finest sculpture will remain in the hills, in the cliffs, undiscovered . . ."

This was not only modesty or confession, it was to a certain extent capitulation as far as some of his ideas and his art of the whole "heroic" period were concerned.

Luckily, among the fragments of the never to be completed *Vidovdan Temple*, besides the stereotyped expression of his didactic ideas, forced stylization in the Oriental manner of past times in which he thought it would be easier to give expression to his ideas, the uncreative repetition of sculpture as a part of architectural effect (the caryatids as columns etc.), all those fragments of the history of a cultural period gone by, there were some masterpieces which have artistic value which rises above the author's ideology.

One of the main figures of the *Vidovdan Temple* was to have been *Kraljević Marko* (1910). This plaster colossus awoke at once admiration and amazement when it was exhibited in Rome in 1911. It was a successful synthesis of Meštrović's art and ideas on the eve of the First World War. It was an embodiment of his conviction of that time "We need to create a cult of the hero!" But here emotion has its firm and healthy sculptural foundation. In that giant statue, which was never again seen full size, but only in the small models made of it, and in the impressive detail of Kraljević Marko's head, there were certain decorative elements reminiscent of von Stuck and Klimt. But while for them this style was their final achievement, on this monumental statue it was only a means to give powerful artistic expression to an idea. We must not neglect this figure, taut with energy, ambition, revolt, ("in spite of non-heroic times"). It is a great shame that it was never cast in bronze for it would be one of the finest modern equestrian statues. *Kraljević Marko* and his horse are a single body, a single compact mass, a single taut muscle a single ambition. They are stylized but they are a synthesis of Euclid's clean and sculpturally justified stylization. In none of the many equestrian statues anywhere in the world, after those of Donatelli and Verrochi, is there such powerful harmony of idea and form, and there is no trace of it in Meštrović's later equestrian monuments either in Yugoslavia or abroad except in his American *Indians*.

What was said of *Kraljević Marko* is true too of *Miloš Obilić* (1908; Belgrade) the second hero of the Kossovo cycle. There is the same forward movement full of energy and daring, the same tenseness, the same logic of stylization which, particularly in this statue, is subordinated to an almost realistic modelling of the muscles. This makes *Miloš Obilić* nearer to Rodin's *Man Walking* but with a monumentality which Rodin in the above sculpture nor even in his *Thinker* never achieved. There is something similar in his *Selfportrait* of 1912, the best of his many selfportraits although the least well known.

Marko and *Miloš* are typical of sculpture formed in plaster, but *Banović Strahinja* (Torso) in the Tate Gallery although also originally conceived as a heroic figure was realized through quite different formal elements. It was one of Meštrović's first big stone sculptures. Very likely he carved it himself in the hard white marble and the material itself dictated less stylization. It has some affinity with the Greek Parthenon figures of the fifth century. There may possibly be some direct influence, but it may also be an expression of the same southern clarity and strength seen in the work of the old Greeks and this Dalmatian.

How basically right and healthy Meštrović's respect for material was (and this is one of the main conditions for good sculpture) is shown by a comparison of *Obilić* and *Strahinja*. The first is created from inwards to outside, the final tense form being gained by the addition of clay. The second is made from a block of stone by the process of reduction, and has retained, (even from the formal point of view for in the base the natural unworked stone has been kept), the elements of the original stone block. A further proof of his feeling for these two opposed materials is that to attain the desired monumentality in *Obilić* Meštrović concentrated on the torso and left out the lower part of the legs and the arms, even the area between the legs is closed. The stone sculpture of Strahinja is even more cubic and static, here there are no arms and legs at all, and not even a head.

Besides making figures in clay which were intended finally to be cast in bronze, Meštrović also worked at this time in stone and for stone. It was his most productive period, and the one in which he made most of his stone sculptures himself, not leaving the final finishing to others except his close collaborater Toma Rosandić. His feeling for stone increased and so did his use of the closed form. From this period date his beautifully modelled fragments *Dancer* (1913; Split), *Mother and Child* (1912; Belgrade) with his own typical stylization, and *My Mother* (1908; Belgrade), a stylized standing torso. These figures despite their symbolical accentuation of line have all the best qualities of a true understanding of stone. In fact only in stone do these figures come to full expression.

At this time Meštrović was doing female nudes too as a complement to his male nudes. Thus alongside *Miloš Obilić* we have *Innocence* (1908; Split) in its simplicity and sensitivity equal to anything by Maillol, though almost unique in the whole range of Meštrović's sculpture. As a foil to *Kraljević Marko* is *Widow* (1908; Belgrade, Split) a figure which in a strange way seems to fuse Rodin's womanliness and Meštrović's manliness. It was intended as one of the widows of the *Vidovdan Temple*, and has all the elements of the "heroic sculpture" that he was then obsessed with, but there is no trace of the forced stylization that we find in the caryatids and the sphinxes. Typical secession traits are noticeable only in the wavy hair, and the emotion of "heroism" realized through enlarged size. The "barbarian" strength of Marko is matched by "barbarian" beauty, accentuated sensuality (suffering around the eyes, an unquenchable sensuality in the half opened mouth) and a promise of fertility. These vigorous marble carvings do not demand to be looked at from any one angle, our eye needs to take them in from various aspects. The roughness of the unworked lower parts only accentuate the wonderful finish of the main part.

There are many similarities of basic conception and style in the other woman's figure that was also originally conceived as one of the Vidovdan widows, and later called *Memories* (1908; Belgrade). In this figure of high sculptural quality there is less of the animal lust for life. Here memory and grief are something more spiritual and inward. Her glance is half turned downwards, her thoughts are on the past while those of the first widow are projected forward towards activity and movement. *Memories* has a lyricism that is rare in Meštrović's Kossovo cycle. This statue too has nothing of the set pose. From every angle a new richness of line and shape is discovered. Under the powerful impression of supressed emotion almost all typical Secession stylization has been forgotton, and the figure is almost exclusively spacially realized.

Unfortunately never again was Meštrović to attain the sculptural purity and beauty of these figures. It was seeing these works that made Rodin exclaim "Meštrović is the greatest phenomenon among sculptors."

After his long years of intensive work on the Kossovo cycle Meštrović took a short journey to Italy, London and was then invited to Vienna to hold a one-man exhibition. Toma Rosandić came to his studio in Vienna and helped him to execute his plaster figures in stone.

In 1909 Meštrović exhibited almost 60 works, most of them fragments of the Kossovo Cycle. He held the exhibition in a separate hall of the Vienna Secession Group and it caused a sensation. In the conservative capital of the Hapsburg Empire it was very daring at that time to show works which had as their theme not only the Slav past but such open allusions to the current political situation. At the entrance to the exhibition were placed two enormous heads, *Kraljević Marko* coloured gold and *Srdje Zlopogledje* coloured red and blue. The posters advertizing the exhibition were equally provoking. It is hardly surprizing that the Crown Prince, Franz Ferdinand forbade the purchase of works which the cultural commission had selected for the Royal Gallery in Belvedere.

Because of the enormous interest it awakened the closing date was twice postponed. The conservative court critics attacked it for its ideas, the art critics and the younger generation were enthusiastic. The whole art world and periodicals proclaimed Meštrović to be the greatest artist in the entire Empire, but at the same time deplored the fact that his inspiration should have been kindled by such a theme as the Serbian past. "If he were a mature man" wrote the Vienna correspondent of *Prager Tagblatt* "who was giving a retrospective exhibition we would feel that we were looking at the results of a very productive artist. But Meštrović is still very young and his productivity is only at its beginning".

The leading art historians Arthur Rossler and Josef Strzygowski wrote eulogies on the twenty-five year old sculptor and called him a "phenomenon". Singling out the national accent and the clear call to revolt in Meštrović's work the German-leaning Strzygowski wrote "We shall be in difficulties if Meštrović's fellow nationals understand his message, and if his art awakes in them new ideas of unity!"

Meštrović moved his entire exhibition to Zagreb, and put before his own people his Kossovo fragments about which so much had been said and written. The exhibition was held in April 1910 and he held it together with his friend, the painter Mirko Račić. The young critics acclaimed the exhibition with enthusiasm, the more conservative with reserve, but after its great success in Vienna no one tried to criticize it.

The same year, in September and October, the Croatian Art Society, "Medulić" organized a big exhibition in the Art Pavilion. For this Meštrović completed his equestrian colossus *Kraljević Marko,* the central figure of the Kossovo Cycle, and studies for the frescoes in the *Vidovdan Temple.* Around Meštrović, and in the shadow of the colossus the other members of the society exhibited: Vlaho Buhovac, Toma Rosandić, Mirko Račić, Ljubo Babić, Tomislav Krizman, Branko Dešković, Emanuel Vidović, Ivan Tišov, Celestin Medović, Nadeža Petrović, Matej Jama, Ivan Grohar, Rihard Jakopič, architects Josip Plečnik, Kamilo Tončić etc. This exhibition mainly gathered together Croatian artists from Dalmatia who did not agree with the official and very "pro-regime" attitude of the Croatian Art Society in Zagreb. The "Medulić" group had put their art at the service of patriotism, and wanted their exhibitions and publications, especially abroad, to contribute to the freedom and unification of all South Slavs. One of the older painters, Vlaho Buhovac, was president of the society, the poet Ivo Vojnović was the ideological leader and Meštrović the most outstanding artist and political personality. The first big collective exhibition staged by the society had been in Split in 1908, the First Dalmatian Art Exhibition. The 1910 exhibition in Zagreb was its second and it was both an art and a political manifestation, held under Vojnović's provocative slogan "Despite unheroic times!". Slovenes and Serbs exhibited as well as Croats.

Meštrović had his greatest success with the statues of his *Kossovo Cycle*, including *Kraljević Marko* at the International Art Exhibition in Rome in 1911. The Austro-Hungarian Ministry had invited him, as their subject, to exhibit in the Austrian pavilion. He replied that as a Croat he did not belong there and declined the invitation. Since the Hungarians were also against the Croats having a separate pavilion at the exhibition Meštrović sent his sculptures to the pavilion of the Kingdom of Serbia, which he and P. Bajalović designed in Secession style. This pavilion became the greatest attraction of the whole exhibition, and Meštrović's sculptures were given first prize. Everyone was impressed with the corridor of Meštrović's caryatids and his enormous *Kraljević Marko* placed in the middle of the pavilion below the cupola and surrounded by reliefs of the figures of warriors.

At this exhibition for the first time Meštrović gained the recognition, support and friendship of the most outstanding progressives of the time. "Magnificent" said the Italian sculptor Leonardo Bistolfi "A new discovery. I shall come again tomorrow and the day after tomorrow and even that will not be enough!". The Milan paper *Corriere della Sera* wrote of him as one of the greatest sculptors of the day who could be compared only to Rodin. In the Rome *Messagera* it wrote "The Serbian Pavilion is the wonder of the Valle Jiulia. Visitors, be they art critics or the ordinary public, leave the pavilion with a deep and unforgettable impression. History and legend are here *alive* — in our times this is incredible. We are faced with art of a new kind, elemental, magnificent, set up in opposition to today's aristocratic Europe which cannot but be bewildered. It has come forth as suddenly as an unexpected trumpet call . . . We know that it is not the *technique* of art that today needs renewing, but its *essence,* if not the decay of our civilization is certain. Ivan Meštrović, this new Homer in stone — this maker of a world created by his chisel, was only fifteen years ago a shepherd in the Dalmatian mountains, today he is almost a Michelangelo."

The famous English painter, John Lavery, writing of *Kraljević Marko* said "This is the most impressive equestrian statue that I have ever seen. It is the general opinion that no European statue on horseback can be compared with the Colleoni in Venice, but I must admit that this *Kraljević Marko* has made a deeper impression on me than the smooth and minutely worked statue of Verrocchia".

Vittorio Pica, in an extensive monograph on the Rome exhibition reserved his highest praise for the works of Meštrović "these powerful and scowling warriors, lonely, suffering widows, these bards impelled by the warmth of their patriotic feelings, these half-naked, deeply sorrowful caryatids borne down by fate, these sphinxes their cold fixed gaze turned to a future imbued with secrets. These are the statues that this young Dalmatian sculptor has conceived for his temple. They are epic, symbolic figures deeply immersed in a spiritual and legendary atmosphere, which gives them a superhuman often hierarchical character. And since, according to the ambitious aims of the sculptor, they must be harmoniously adapted to architectural ends, it was natural that he sought his examples in stylized archaic Assyrian Egyptian or ancient Greek sculpture. It is to these that his and his fellow students' longings and warm admiration have turned, almost as a fruit of hate for all that their teachers at the Art Academy in Vienna tried to get them to admire and to copy."

Giovanni Papini, one of the leading Italian writers, was enthusiastic about Meštrović and later became very friendly with him. For him this sculpture was a breath of fresh air blowing through decadent Europe. The famous Italian painter and writer Ardengo Soffici saw in Meštrović a genius who had managed to combine Eastern art with modern European. The leader of the Italian futurists, F. T. Marinetti, found Meštrović's art had affinities with the movement of which he was the main spirit. The critic Ugo Ojetti acknowledged that Meštrović's works opened up new dimensions in sculpture and destroyed the academic approach. Benedetto Croce alone saw in Meštrović the expression of barbarism. His works at the Rome exhibition made Maxim Gorky enthusiastic. He came to know Meštrović in Rome in 1911 and was proud that a Slav had made such a powerful impact on the art life of Europe.

As he had a considerable number of commissions Meštrović remained in Rome for two years. He had a small flat in via Babuino, a centre of the art and literary world of that time. Most of the day he spent in his studio in Via Flaminia near the Piazza del Popolo. He had many friends, among them Vittorio Pica, the sculptor Leonardo Bistolfi, and the Spanish painter

Anglada y Camarasa. It was at this time that he made his big wooden model of the *Vidovdan Temple*, and continued to work on his sculptures for it. Because of the reception of his work at the Rome exhibition, and the fact that he had exhibited in the Serbian Pavilion, from this time on the Austrian government kept constant watch on him.

In 1913 he made a short visit to London, drawn by his desire to see Pheidias's sculptures for the Parthenon in the British Museum. After that he went to Belgrade and received a commission for a fountain to commemorate the victory of the Serbian army in the Balkan wars. This *Monument to Freedom* was supposed to have been put up in the middle of Belgrade Terazija. Meštrović conceived it in the form of a huge basin supported by four lions, and from its centre a column would rise surmounted by the figure of the *Victor*. Around the column would be masks through which water would pour into the basin.

For nine months he worked on this project, but the outbreak of war interrupted him. The *Monument to Freedom* remained unfinished, and during the war many of his works were destroyed. All that was left of the monument was the bronze figure of the *Victor*, in the classical style of Hildebrand. After the war this was mounted on a high column and placed in Kalemegdan Park, Belgrade, where still today it dominates the silhouette of the city.

Meštrović spent the 1914—1918 war years in emigration, working at his sculpture and very active in the political field for the freedom and unification of the South Slavs.

He was in Venice when the Sarajevo assassination took place. He immediately took a boat to Split where he was due to hold an exhibition of his Kossovo sculpture. He was warned that the Austrian government intended to arrest and intern him and the other leaders of the nationalist movement. He managed to escape to Italy and went to live in Rome. Here, together with his fellow political emigrants Ante Trumbić, Fran Supilo etc. he began intensive propaganda for South Slav freedom and unification. The Allies in the secret London Agreement of 1915 had promised Italy to give her Dalmatia if she went into the war on their side. Many Serbian politicians were interested only in a greater Serbia and indifferent to the idea of uniting with the Croats and Slovenes. In 1914 the emigrants founded the Yugoslav Committee with its seat in London. For the whole war period Meštrović was a very active member of that committee. He tried to use his fame in the field of art, and kept alive by exhibitions held during the war, to contribute to the national idea. When opinion in Italy became very anti-Croat, because of their designs on Dalmatia, Meštrović moved to Paris, and then to London where the seat of the committee was. The British took him in with great warmth and belped him in his patriotic work. Not only his personal popularity, but sympathy for the Yugoslav national question were hehind the exhibitions which he held in 1915 in London and later in other British towns. In 1916 he was in the South of France, in Nice and Cannes. The same year he lived and did a considerable amount of wood carving in Geneva. In 1917 he returned to London and again held an exhibition there. When the end of the war came it found him ill in Switzerland.

During the war a number of important exhibitions of his work were held in Great Britain. The one that aroused most attention was held in the Victoria and Albert Museum in summer 1915. A whole group of British artists, writers, politicians and other public figures, led by Seton Watson, did everything they could not only to spread the fame of Meštrović as a sculptor, but also to call attention and awaken sympathy for the South Slav nations, who on all battlefields at that time seemed to be doing badly. Meštrović was especially honoured as his exhibition was the first that this famous museum had ever arranged of the works of a living artist. This in its turn called up the opposition of the conservatives, which all increased the popularity of the exhibition and the patriotic ideas behind it.

The Victoria and Albert Exhibition was opened by Lord Robert Cecil, assistant Minister of Foreign Affairs. Enthusiastic notices of it were written by leading British art critics and artists James Bone, Sir John Lavery, Ernest Collings, P. G. Konody, John Murray, Frank Rutter, C. H. Collins-Baker and others. After London the sculptures were shown in Leeds, and Glasgow, later (1918) in Bradford, again in Glasgow and Edinburgh where the Royal Scottish Academy elected him a member. In London also, in 1918, he held two more exhibitions, one in the Twenty-one Gallery, the other in the premises of the Serbian Red Cross, the last of these being opened by the famous English painter Frank Brangwyn.

In the years just before the war Meštrović had been obsessed with ideas of national freedom and the unification of the South Slavs. As he himself admitted this political belief almost became an art programme. It suited his heroic sculptures, and his emotional presentation and was behind the forced ideas of "nationalism" and "barbarism" then basic to much of his work. If there was any religious note at that time at all it was an expression of his mystical "Vidovdan faith". With the coming of war his whole obsession with Kossovo disappeared, even patriotic subjects disappeared, although his homeland was not free, and he was an emigrant in Rome, Paris and London. In place of idealistic patriotism, humanistic religious preoccupation now came uppermost. Even in his first works Meštrović had inclined towards reflective and humanistic ideas, concerned almost with ontological problems. This was the impact of many of Rodin's sculptures, and even more the influence of the reflective work of the later Tolstoy, and also to a certain extent memories left in his mind from hearing the Bible in his youth.

His national enthusiasm had for a time suppressed these ideas. He seemed now to have sufferered a certain disappointment with art too narrowly ideologically directed. A period of self-criticism began, the apprehension that the artistic realization of many of his great and strongly felt ideas had too often produced little more than work on the level of posters and scenery. He came to believe that a universal human faith was more important than race or nationality. These feelings were reinforced by the slaughter of war, absurd, unromantic and anti-heroic in essence and detail. A general disillusionment with great emotional ideals and a return to the inner, individual world of feeling are behind Meštrović's later assertions of the relativity of art:

The real guide is faith . . . when we try to find total harmony in what we call justice, truth, beauty, wisdom, divided like this they glimmer like fireflies and are gone.

Or even more definite:

That is why we should not allow our feelings to be attracted to generalized human sentiments in the spiritual sense, nor by the phraseology of nationalism.

The world war was a terrible disappointment for mankind. Its pointlessness and destruction drove old Rodin to despair and finally to death in 1918. It had a decisive effect on Meštrović. Passivity took the place of action, the static that of the dynamic, contemplation that of heroism. His figures no longer look forward into the future but rather look into themselves, into the drama taking place within and which is no less than the outer world drama.

His nationalism ceased to be a prophetic call to action, it became political and diplomatic and had little direct effect on the artist within. After the war he tried to justify his work:

Immediately after the Balkan War, and especially after the World War, it seemed to me that the ideals of a single nation were too little, the sacrifices or victory of a single nation of not great enough significance in comparison with the sacrifices and victory of all. But this general victory can be achieved only if there are no "friends" and "enemies", if we all become brothers and people. It was thinking about these ideas that brought me to biblical themes. A feeling for the general suffering of man took the place that until then had been filled by a feeling for the suffering of my own nation . . ."

Whether in Rome, Paris or London Meštrović fully realized all the horrors of those bloody war years. Millions of people killed, the culture of centuries destroyed, and worst of all — so many ideals shattered too. It led to a fundamental change in his spiritual life and in his artistic expression.

A close acquaintance from the war years in London, Director of the Gallery of Modern Art in the British Museum, James Bone, described the change as follows: "Meštrović's art was not apart from his life. He is one of the few artists in history whose art was dedicated to his country... In his youth he mourned for the past; in his maturity he had to mourn the present. The tragic atmosphere of his nation's destiny falls around all his work."

The same kind of account is given by one of his closest friends, the painter Jozo Kljaković, who was close to him during all the war years: "In those difficult war years (1914—1918) and in the choking reek of human blood, he turned away from the heroes of the sword and towards the heroes of the spirit. The first figure was his *Christ on the Cross* and a number of carved wooden panels showing the life of Christ, including a *Virgin and Child.* All these were wood carvings. Except for a few portraits which he did in London and one penitent little girl at prayer, he did little else during the war except these details from the Life of Christ. So deeply did the horror of war shake him."

That strange, and for Meštrović unusual, almost Moorelike *Pieta* (1914) in Split is the most obvious and the most impressive proof of his spiritual preoccupations at that time. The change from the self-confidence, and drive of his *Selfportrait* (1912) is startling. Christ's face in this small sculpture is not completely defined. But only a little later in *Head of Christ* (1914; Split) and *St. John the Baptist* (1914; Zagreb Belgrade) there is a tragic expression, artistically conservative with overtones of Gothic expression.

The height of this Gothic, expressive mysticism, of all embracing humanism was reached in his huge *Crucifixion* (1917) carved in wood in Geneva and today in his *Kaštelet* in Split. With no fixed studio, especially after he had to leave Rome for London, Meštrović worked a lot in wood during the war. He made reliefs of biblical scenes, among them the first of his series of wooden panels for the cycle *The Life of Christ* (Split). These vary greatly in style and quality. He concentrated so hard on expression that he often tended to forget plastic values.

There are two main reason's for the Gothic influence and exaggerated stylization of this time. One is because of his feeling of man's helplessness and suffering and his turning towards transcendental values. This led him to carve elongated shapes, especially arms and legs, symbolic fingers, unrealistic draperies, the stress laid on the main features and the lesser ones neglected.

The second source of this style was the technique by which he conceived his wood carvings. Earlier he had modelled his original sketches in clay and from the first had been conscious of volume. Now, without the intermediary stage in clay or plaster, he drew his sketches, full-size on paper. The conception was graphic not plastic and when he transferred it from paper to wood he sometimes did it almost mechanically.

There is an ancient element in mankind's longings which makes him feel a similarity between a tree trunk and his own body. Any forcing of wood which goes against the material itself has a negative effect on sculpture. For this reason the large size of the wooden panels was not always a happy solution. It often led to superficial finish of all parts, or difficulties in the composition of the figures. This was the more so as the central figure of Christ was in the form of a long vertical and the various panels were partly controlled by their place in the cycle as a whole. When Meštrović in a "breathing space" between the two wars carved on some left-over, uneven panels he adapted himself to his material to its hardness and graining, and the results were on a much higher level.

The best fusion of intention, form and material is without doubt the *Crucifixion* in the *Kaštelet*. Its vertical lines are accentuated, human body and tree trunk are one, and visually and spiritually it symbolizes the idea of transcendental suffering and martyrdom. There is nothing monotonous in the verticals. Harmony and rhythm have been achieved by the unnatural but expressive spread of the arms to form a V shape, the head bent towards the right shoulder. Christ's body clearly shows the marks of the chisel and how much the sculptor understood the nobility of the material in which he was working. The stylization and unnatural size did not get in the way of a truly sculptural treatment of volume. The same cannot be said for many of the reliefs of that and the later period.

The sculptor's son, Mate, has given an interesting explanation of the close connection between his father's work and his deepest personal feelings, in which the *Crucifixion* played a particularly important part: ''I often think that his works are the truest expression of his spirit. Into hundreds of figures, done over a period of more than sixty years, he carved the torrent of his emotions, his faith and his hopes, his understanding of himself and his surroundings, the mysticism of his maturity and old age. — His horror at the lying slogans which called on millions to lay down their lives in the world war is expressed in the huge exhausted and twisted body of the *Crucifixion* which he did in 1917. It was not the intention of this *Crucifixion* he wrote later, to show the Christ of history, but to be a realization of the Christian ideal within man.''

Of the *Crucifixion* James Bone just before the end of the war wrote these moving words: ''You can see that this Christ has been a long time on the Cross. Centuries have gone by and the spiritual renaissance has still not taken place in Man's heart. Brutality still strides through the world, head high. Whole nations are being crucified and blood is flowing pitilessly throughout Europe. This is not realistic art, but it has the terrible reality of an artist who has personally experienced the death agony of body and spirit and gives us passionate and agonizing witness of the fact that crucifixion is not something that took place when the world was young, it is still terribly relevant to us — children of the twentieth century . . .''

Only a few of the carved panels in *Kaštelet* reach this high quality of fusion of graphic and sculptural elements. There is something lyric, almost musical, in those where line and surface treatment are predominant, while those in which the carving is deeper make a more dramatic effect. The lyrical feeling is present in one of the very first panels carved *Virgin and Angels* (1917). Lack of depth is not felt in this case because the subject itself is a truly lyrical one, and the repetition of the angel's heads does not make for monotony but provides a special rhythm. The *Annunciation* (1927) is a similar panel of high artistic quality. A harmonious composition of verticals and diagonals brings out the theme to the full. The whole composition, figures and details, is both full of meaning and artistically functional. *Jesus and the Woman of Samaria* (1927) in particular stands out with its happy arrangement of line and mass and its wonderful contrast, from both the sculptural and human angle, of the ascetic body of Christ and the rounded, almost erotic body of the woman.

Similar critical principles can be applied to Meštrović's other religious sculpture of the same period. When he fully took into account the material in which he was working he obtained a very successful synthesis of form and meaning. Among his many statues of the *Virgin and Child* he achieved successful composition and discreet stylization in *Virgin Riding* (1917) in Split Gallery, and the particularly fine and sensitive wooden *Virgin* in the Zagreb Studio (1917). A complete feeling for the wood which he was carving, and the fine workmanship of head and hands, make this sculpture one of Meštrović's best and most ''modern''. He was similarly successful in his *Angel with a Flute* (1918) in Zagreb Modern Art Gallery. The elongated soft modelling makes the bronze seem to live, and the fact that the flute is only suggested by the position of the fingers gives this statue a special poetry and melodiousness.

In these productive war years abroad besides sculptures, almost mystical in their stylization, he did a whole series of realistic if idealized statues and busts of women which are among his finest of their kind. There is *Ruža Meštrović* (1915; Split, Zagreb), *Women Praying* (1917; Split), *Vestal Virgin* (1917; Split) and the girls with musical instruments of 1918; *Distant music* (1918; Split), *Girl with a Lute* (1918; Zagreb). In the fine stylization of these last he poured all his feeling for music, lyricism and restrained symbolism. The carving is not deep, and detail is reduced to the minimum, they have similarities with his religious subjects though they do not share their reflective mysticism and drama. Strangely enough an enormous joy in life, clear pure classicism with a western refinement of feeling radiates from these women's forms and these musical girls. It is present in facial expression, in the movement of fingers and arms, the soft, simply moulded body lines. It was in these figures that Meštrović, dynamic peasant sculptor of heightened emotion, differed most from his earlier style and was closest to the contemporary sculpture of Despiau, Lipschitz and Lawrence. There was probably no direct influence from these sculptors. Perhaps one source of these elongated lines, the liesurely elegance of the figures, might be found in the life which Meštrović was living at that time in the salons of Rome and London, and the fame which he had acquired, perhaps too in a satiety with heroic and monumental forms and with religious problems. The most direct influence however was certainly his discovery of the gracious beauty of the Italian pre-Renaissance painters, and the English Pre-Raphaelites. Melodiousness and intimacy, as opposed to drama and monumentality, were always a component in Meštrović's art. The harmoniousness and melodiousness of these figures was meant to be a reflection of a general human harmony. ("It was longing for general harmony that was behind my newest works, those with musićal and melodious motifs"). Luckily he expressed this in the visual rather than the metaphysical field.

Among almost 70 works by Meštrović done in the war years, and now scattered all over the world, mostly in Italy and Britain, there was the interesting relief *The Archers of Domogoj* (1917), today in the collection of Professor H. Seton Watson in London. This relief was supposed to be the first of a new series of reliefs, a Croatian cycle, like his Kossovo cycle but the idea was born and died in this single work.

In the interwar period (1918—1941) Ivan Meštrović was a famous man in the public life of his own country. He did not directly take part in politics but was at the centre of most political happenings. The freedom and unification of the South Slav nations brought more disappointment than enthusiasm. The ideals of the pre-war nationalistic youth were muddied by the Belgrade establishment (the *čaršija*) and various political careerists. In the new monarchy all nationalities did not get equal freedom and justice and this meant continual disagreement and struggle. In his disappointment with the Yugoslav ideal Meštrović now sought relief in the development of the Croatian national consciousness. He propagated the idea publicly and in his works. Part of his disappointment lay in the fact that he was not able to bring to fruition some of his ideas. His plan for the *Vidovdan Temple* was as complete a failure as were the ideals of the prewar youth. Narrow, middle-class conceptions of art made it impossible for him to put into effect his plans for the interior of the new church of St. Blazius in Zagreb. His wartime *Crucifixion,* one of his most powerful works, was rejected by clergy and laity alike because of its expressionism. In the same way his large wood-carved panels showing the *Life of Christ,* which he had intended to place round the church walls, under frescoes to be done by his friend Jozo Kljaković, were also considered unacceptable. Finally his scheme of founding a private Academy of Art in Zagreb, together with Rosandić, Rački and Križman also failed and these men, friends in good and bad times, now had disagreements.

After two decades of wandering in the capitals of Europe Meštrović now wanted a more settled way of life and work. He bought a small decaying baroque house in the Upper Town in Zagreb and reconditioned it for living and working in. He added a studio and a private courtyard surrounded by columns. He had no children by his first wife and in 1923 he married again, Olga Kesterčanek, who he had met in Dubrovnik while working on the Račić memorial in nearby Cavtat.

He became rector of the Art School, later the Art Academy, in Zagreb and in the next two decades brought up several generations of sculptors, some of whom later became famous Croatian artists. Living and working in Zagreb, the capital of Croatia, he wished to show:

"that this small corner of the world is just as near to, or just as far from, the forces that move the world as any other, in fact for me it is nearer than any other. I believe that each one of us needs to work in our own country, among our own people, giving from ourselves and of ourselves..."

At this time Meštrović took active part in almost all cultural movements in Croatia: in the founding of the Gallery of Modern Art and the New Art Pavilion in Zagreb, organizing the preservation of cultural monuments of the Old Croatian period in Knin, making and donating statues of famous historical personages to many towns, giving his aid in the rebuilding and decorating of St. Mark's Church in Zagreb, Zvonimir's Church in Biskupija etc. The exhibitons that he held in many foreign centres not only made his art more widely known but also the art of his people, until then hardly heard of in the contemporary world, and whose affirmation was particularly necessary because of the irredentist aspirations of her neighbours, particularly those on the Adriatic.

Even when the peace conference was being held in 1919 he organized in Paris a Yugoslav Art Exhibition in the Little Palace des Beaux-Arts. One aim of this was to be a kind of "cultural identity-card" as there were many who tried to prove that the Balkan nations were barbarians. For the exhibition Meštrović tried to get all leading artists in Croatia, Slovenia and Serbia to take part, but it was his own works that were the main attraction and made the greatest effect. The most outstanding names of French cultural and political life were on the honorary committee, among others: Bartholomé, Bourdelle, Matisse, Barbusse, Barrès, Bergson, Loti, Régnier, Diehl, Kahn, Michel etc. A comprehensive preface to the catalogue was written by the art historian André Michel. The figures of the *Kossovo Cycle* and his wooden *Christ* amazed the European public once again.

Meštrović's next breakthrough in the art world were his one-man exhibitions in London (1924, and 1925) New York and other American towns.

The intellectual world of London already knew Meštrović and his earlier work very well, especially that of the war years and it welcomed him back again. In the Fine Arts Gallery, New Bond Street he showed about fifty of his smaller works.

Meštrović had been invited to exhibit in Buffalo in 1912, after Rodin and Meunier, but it was just then that the Balkan War broke out and the exhibition, already loaded on a ship, had to be unloaded. This time he spent nine months in America exhibiting in the Brooklyn Museum, New York, The Art Institute in Chicago, and also in Buffalo, Detroit, Rochester, and Philadelphia. He presented a wide choice of his work from 1906 onwards, all in all 106 sculptures and twenty-one lithographs. He included a large model of the unrealized *Vidovdan Temple*, eight figures from the *Kossovo Cycle*, and a considerable number of religious works from the war years. Christian Brinton, one of the most outstanding art critics of his generation, organized the exhibition and catalogue. He clearly placed Meštrović's art in the framework of contemporary world sculpture, not claiming any *avant-garde* elements in it:

"The position occupied by Ivan Meštrović in contemporary art is midway between the conservatives and the restless, questing radicals. It is, relatively speaking, the position maintained by the Frenchman Maillol, and the Anglo-American Jacob Epstein. With the Yugoslav artist simplicity of line and mass is not pushed so far as is the case with Archipenko, Boccioni, or Lipschitz. The work of Meštrović remains well within the province of readily recognized theme and subject. Simple motifs, heroic, religious, and contemplative, dictate their special forms and media to an art that has won its place in the plastic procession of the ages, an art at once noble and vehement, ardently nationalistic yet possessing a broad and sincere universality of appeal."

It was at this time that Meštrović met Mihajlo Pupin in America, who compared his art to national poetry, and Nikola Tesla, and he received a commission to make the *American Indians* in Chicago. He had further one-man exhibitions in New York in 1927 and 1930 and gained great recognition in spite of the disposition among American intellectuals for *avant-garde* art.

Two extremely important exhibitions of his work between the wars were those in Jeu de Paume in Paris (1933) and in the Belvedere in Prague. The Paris exhibition was under the patronage of M. A. de Monzia, Minister of Education. His special interest in Meštrović's work grew out of his wartime friendship with Rodin and Bourdelle. A catalogue with a very detailed account of the life and work of the sculptor was written for the Paris exhibition by R. Warnier, Director of the French Institute in Zagreb. 63 sculptures and 28 drawings were exhibited. From Paris the exhibition was sent to Prague and shown with enormous success in the Belvedere and the surrounding park.

Meštrović naturally had many exhibitions in his own country, in Zagreb and Ljubljana in 1920 and again in 1923, in Zagreb in 1932. The last of these was to a certain extent a retrospective exhibition of postwar work, his ideals and disillusionment. For the disillusionment increased. Instead of the idea of Yugoslavia there was a dictatorship, and Croatian nationalism was broken by internal friction. There was a world of difference between the enthusiastic and forward looking exhibition of young artists held in 1910 under the parole "Despite unheroic times" and that now held in the same pavilion. The new exhibition was tame, even resigned — "This time", wrote Meštrović in the catalogue "it is not despite" anyone or anything, neither the times nor lack of heroism. Time has equalized us with others, or others with us; there has been too much heroism, — it is still with us, but of humanity there is no sign. Perhaps we should say: "despite our illusions, or despite everything that our white town is not."

He began to be criticized for the express nationalism, religion and emotion of his work. This was linked to the whole criticism of Secession as a failure, as decorative and unoriginal (a judgement that only since the Second World War has been corrected). Yugoslav nationalists attacked Meštrović because of his increasing withdrawal into Croatian nationalism; the socialistically inclined intellectuals, particularly M. Pijade and M. Krleža, criticized the religious factor in his art, though Miroslav Krleža said that his works had an absolute value, regardless of what message they carried. But nobody could dimish his position as the best known contemporary Croatian and Yugoslav artist, the only one famous outside his own country.

This was the period of his maturity. He was highly thought of and in great demand both at home and abroad. Besides a whole gallery of world famous personalities he was responsible for monuments to national leaders and rulers all over Yugoslavia and abroad. This gave him a great feeling of confidence in his work, and allowed him to make large-sized monuments and buildings; but the extent of his activity, the speed at which he worked, and the technical difficulties of individual statues did not allow time for the artist within him to ripen, nor did it permit him to distance himself from what he was doing and develop self-criticism. In addition he could not himself carry through all phases of the work. In too many cases the creative process was confined to the drawing or sketches he made on paper.

After that it was more or less a technical matter often done by his pupils or professional stone-masons under his control. This is especially true of many shallow reliefs, big architectural and sculptural monuments and the wooden reliefs of his biblical cycle. He began to be further and further removed from the final material in which the work was carried out and made an increasing number of things in plaster, later to have them carved in stone or cast in bronze, and occasionally unfortunately both. In rare moments he found time to work directly on stone once more doing uncommissioned work with no set theme. It was as if the true artist within, so often cramped and suffocated, needed space to breathe. Projecting his ideas on paper or executing them, usually by incising and not modelling in clay, he often lost the feel for sculpture as a special art, and too great a stress on philosophical, national or religious ideas meant a loss of plastic values. On the plane of ideas, always so important for a study of Meštrović's work, the feeling for general human problems began to give place more and more to an expression of religious and national feelings in the narrower sense. Most of his new works had these ideas behind them. Although they were no longer romantic in the same way that the *Kossovo Cycle* at the beginning of the century had been romantic, they still remained basically romantic in conception and expression: glorification of the national past; symbolic heralding of the future; patriarchal, active, religious life, usually biblically robed; a patriarchal and national accentation of his peasant origins; the family as the basis of society; the church as the repository of tradition and culture. As one might logically expect, now that he had come to maturity and taking into account his pre-war political aspirations, he made huge monuments of various famous national figures: *Marko Marulić* (1924; Split), *Andrija Medulić* (Zagreb), *Bishop Gregory of Nin*, (Split) *Josip Juraj Strossmayer* (Zagreb), *King Peter* (1930; Dubrovnik), *French Memorial* (1930; Belgrade), *Rudjer Bošković* (Zagreb), monuments of Romanian rulers etc. In these monuments he seldom achieved the happy synthesis of form style and idea that he had in his uncast *Kraljević Marko*. It was as if something rational and dogmatic interrupted the spontaneous impulse of modelling and of direct expression in the round. Meštrović even formulated certain principles concerning statuary sculpture, he took something from his own personal experience, something from the new approach to sculpture and something from a combination of Bourdelle's monumental art and Hildebrand's sculpture as part of the general architectural effect. In 1937 he wrote: "Only today do I see the important role of architecture in sculpture, and to what extent we sculptors are handicapped when we want to compose a more widely conceived piece of art and have no architectural experience."

As opposed to the realistic and naturalistic approach to sculpture for statues of the earlier century, and the impressionistic-intimate approach of Rodin's period, Meštrović's conception was based on a reduction of detail and strong stress on the basic idea of the monument. For him a statue was something like a poster: it should be immediately understood, both from the point of view of its form and of its message. One characteristic of his figures done according to this scheme is their position. They often have an unnatural stance the purpose of which is to make the underlying idea completely clear and unmistakable. The form is dictated by the desire that the statue should make an instantaneous effect from a certain angle, and not be gradually discovered as a creation in the round. The monuments are usually made to give an effect from profile view, and have an accented forward movement to attain which he often twists the figure in the upper part of the body. These monuments usually make a wonderfully impressive effect at first sight which makes them very popular. But after a slightly longer and more detailed analysis there seems to be a certain emptiness, lack of detail a searching for momentary effect. The main weakness of these statues is their lack of plasticity. They were designed to achieve an effect through a silhouette, the gaze fixed in a certain direction. Part of the reason for this is that they were conceived to be placed in certain special surroundings and their stance and composition was conditioned by these (a typical example is *Bishop Gregory of Nin* designed to stand in the Peristyle in Split).

When the surroundings were happily chosen such statues make a momentary, unforgettable impression, but in other cases, where they stand in the middle of surroundings of a different art period and style, particularly in historically conditioned localities, they cannot acclimatize themselves, and always run the risk that their huge dimensions break up the existing style of their surroundings.

Some of Meštrović's huge statues have been destroyed by time, some will remain as a reminder of a certain cultural-historical period and of the personality of Meštrović. But there are some that have greatness in their own right. For example *Bishop Gregory of Nin* in Split (1926—27) is one of Meštrović's finest monuments, although the effect is largely confined to one angle, profile. There is sculptural reason behind the simple masses of this bronze colossus. The smooth folds of the clothing achieve a rhythm of their own, they accentuate the height and impressive monumentality of the figure, and the curved almost windblown effect of the upper garments give an impression of fierce temperament. The statue of *Josip Juraj Strossmayer* in Zagreb (1926) is not so obviously monumental but it has greater plasticity is more true to sculptural principles and can be approached from any angle.

Meštrović's finest monumental sculptures are his Chicago *Indians* (1926—27), they are not too obviously stylized: the muscles of the horsemen are almost anatomically realistic. The basic idea and monumentality is not achieved by size and simplification of detail (for even the models of these sculptures give an effect of monumentality, as does *Kraljević Marko*) but by cleaness of line and a splendid use of diagonals beginning low at the back of the statues and projected forward and upward to produce a wonderful unity of horse and rider, even though the size of the horse would make it easy for it to predominate. In these figures Meštrović did not have drapery to help him as he usually did, and he was forced to make use of his old knowledge of the human body. These statues show how much more important true sculptural feeling is than ideology, for Meštrović hardly knew anything about the ideals of the American Indian and they certainly did not move him, although he felt in these Indian horsemen something of his never to be finished statue of *Kraljević Marko*.

A number of Meštrović's other small inter-war sculptures have affinities with the monuments mentioned above for example *Michelangelo* (1925; Italy), *Goethe* (1930; Split, Zagreb), and his celebrated *Selfportrait* (1926, Split). They all seek to make an emotional effect and have similarly unnatural body positions used to produce it. They are the result of Meštrović's veneration for Michelangelo and Goethe (as he had once venerated Tolstoy). The selfportrait shows a considerable feeling of self-confidence. Another statue in this same genre is his *Croatian History* (1932, Zagreb, Belgrade), a very successful synthesis between allegory and stylized from. The folk motif is reduced to the minimum, clothing is used to increase the impression desired in a way rarely successful even in his sculpture. The tranquillity, symmetry and balance of horizontals and verticals give a wonderfully impressive figure. It was intended for a still unbuilt museum of Croatian Archeological Antiquities.

Some of Meštrović's finest inter-war works are his marble nudes of women. The rectangular shape that he so often used give them massivity but at the same time he achieved softness in line and volume. There is a southern sensuality in the full forms of the body and a spirituality in their tranquil contemplation. These sculptures are the products of a mature artist, at the height of his physical and mental powers. They suggest a physiological and esthetic impulse a compensating for his ideological, religious, symbolic and mystical preoccupations. They are a flight to the natural, to classical purism, and the temperament of the south. They mean a return to sculptural values often neglected in his other work, and a true joy in the marble in which he was working. The architectonics of sculpture here come to full expression, "there are no free figures which do not have their roots in architecture". (Volfflin). If we compare some of the wooden reliefs of the same period with these sculptures it is difficult to believe that they were done by the same man.

Contemplation (1923; Split), is a statue conceived in marble. Cast in bronze it would not be nearly as fine as carved in stone. In *Psyche* (1927; Split) Meštrović reached the height of his artistic expression. It is form truly sculpturally conceived. Each detail has been carefully considered and harmonized with the whole. The fine and detailed work on the surface does not in the least detract from the strength of the basically cubic structure. If we sought for an analogy in the history of sculpture we might most nearly find it in Pheidias's figures on the acropolis or Michelangelo's figures on the tombs of the Medicis.

Another step forward in freeing himself from outer forms of stylization are to be found in the reclining female nudes *Dreaming* (1927; Split), *Resting* (1929; Split), *Waiting* (1929; Zagreb), *Woman Beside the Sea* (1926; Zagreb) *Woman's Torso* (1940; Split). In spite of their obvious realism he did not always feel it necessary to ''round off'' the forms — so great was his mastery of sculpture and so monumental and yet at the same time lyrical was his creation. It is difficult to say whether this was an effect of Maillol or the Czech Šturse, or whether there was some reciprocal influence between him and young Kršinić, a master of marble nudes (or did they have some common source). It is a fact however that Meštrović's works are ''more monumental'' than Maillol's, firmer in purpose than Šturse's and more full of temperament than Kršinić's. Their particular attraction lies in the match of mass and material, the smooth, white, hard marble on the rough carving of the chiselled bases. In fact Meštrović did not do the actual stone carving himself, but from the very first moment, through sketch and model he felt their final form in marble. The majority can be looked at from all sides, even from the back, and no single static line of vision is taken for granted. These works are not conceived in the two dimensional relief of the painter. In his *Indians* Meštrović gave free rein to his desire for the monumental, here he freed himself from all the ballast of the need to represent ideas and allowed himself to express lyricism and joy in life and work in the wonderful material that Pheidias and Michelangelo had used. While most of his stylized sculptures, especially those of a public character, demand a special setting these have a life apart from their surroundings. They fit equally well into indoor halls, in the green of parks and gardens, under brilliant sunshine, with no fear that they will be deprived of any of their value as works of art. Indeed they often seen like part of nature, like the forms of living rock or pieces of volcanic stone. Their links with elemental nature come to particular expression in the life and sun of the open air.

At this same time he did a number of statues of women playing musical instruments. In comparison with the above nudes they seem to be raised to a level above reality.
The basic musical idea and the metaphysics of a greater harmony are not only achieved by the inclusion of some musical instrument but by the treatment of the whole. There is much more stylization here, stress of abstract rhythm in the movement of the clothing, idealized facial expression, unrealistic treatment of the fingers, the sculpture worked out as a whole rather than in details through accented shallow relief. When he did not take into full enough account the sculptural possibilities of the material in which the figure was to be made the creative stages of such reliefs were often ended with the artist's sketch which was more or less mechanically transferred without him playing any great part in it. But when he consciously had in mind carved or modelled figures then these musical women and girls are not far in quality behind the statues of women mentioned above. Indeed in a certain spirituality and musicality they surpass them. Such marble reliefs are *Girl with a Lute* (1927; London) and *Woman with a Harp* (1930) in the entrance porch of Meštrović's Split villa, and some others.

Meštrović conceived these musical figures often more rationally than he did esthetically. ''My newest things with musical and melodic motifs (1933) have grown out of a longing for general harmony. They are an expression of my feeling and longing for harmony between us and the whole world. If we succeed at least at moments to achieve harmony between us and all that is around us and above us, it is something. One day those will come who will achieve lasting harmony."

But, although we need not deny the importance of the idea of general harmony, this is not what first strikes us as we stand in the sunny gardens of Meštrović's villa in Split and look at *Distant Music*, or stand in its classical porch to look at the relief *Woman with a Harp*. Our basic feelings are those of wonder at the beauty and the harmony of these women's bodies, the movement, line, composition, youth, gentleness and a certain charm. Only with difficulty do we come to think of the allegorical significance they had for the artist.

Some of the realistic beauty of the marble nudes, especially in the soft treatment of the face, and some of the idealized spirituality and melodiousness of the musical statues is to be found in the many statues of the *Madonna and Child* of this same period. The realism of form allows us to experience these as mothers and as a personification of mother love. A certain idealization in the composition, elements of cold symbolism and the stylization of draperies make them the repositories of religious ideas, women who are not fulfilled with a life of their own, as are the women of the nudes, but women whose meaning is in life outside them, life entrusted to them. Such are: *The Virgin and Children* (1925—26; Split) with the softness of Leonardo, the ascetic *A Mother Dedicates her Child* (1927; Split) growing out of its stone block, the lyrical and dramatic *Magdalena Beneath the Cross* (1919; Zagreb). A little earlier came the Gothic stylization of *Madonna and Child* from the *Virgin of the Angels* (1920—22) in Cavtat, and almost more medieval in expression the bronze *A Mother Teaching her Child to Pray* (England) and the impressive bronze *Pieta* in St. Mark's, Zagreb. In all these religious works Meštrović was realizing his humane and metaphysical ideas. There are other works similar in theme from the same period, usually in shallow relief, more "engraved" than carved, not much more than good drawings carried out in plaster, bronze, wood or stone. The bronze reliefs in the inside of the Račić memorial chapel in Cavtat best show this rational, cold and dogmatic approach, almost that of the draftsman, in spite of the fact that Strzygowski wrote a panegyric about their "traditional" and "national" expression.

Although Meštrović in his long and productive life was greatly concerned with religious themes, from both Old and New Testament, nevertheless we do not feel his religion to have been of the narrowly dogmatic kind. It was more belief in the wider sense than it was religion in the narrower. He himself wrote: "From the point of view of nationality what was and still is important for me is race not belief, and in the religious sense — the humane and the human regardless of Catholic, Orthodox, Protestant or Muslim, or even Buddhist. I see a basic identity in all religions, in their essence that is . . . Everywhere God's truth is the same . . ." It is others who have used Meštrović's works in a partisan spirit in the most varied and even in opposite political programmes.

We can only explain certain apparent contradictions in Meštrović's work if we cease to take too much account of their ideological opposition: for example in the war years his *Christ* on the Cross as an expression of the deliverance of mankind and the prophetic figure of *Lenin* (1924) which equally symbolized faith in and love for man's future.

In the period between the wars Meštrović designed a number of buildings in which sculpture was an important part. His first post-war work of this kind was the *Račić Family Memorial Chapel* or *Our Lady of the Angels* in Cavtat (1920—23). He had been friendly from his London days with the Račić family all of whom died in an epidemic. But quite apart from the personal feelings with which he approached the building and decoration of this chapel it was an expression of his new approach to art, a crystallization of the tragedy of the war years and of emigration. National mysticism gave place to religious mysticism.

Older stylistic elements are to be seen in certain Byzantine and eastern elements in the architecture and the interior and in still present echoes of Secession.

The chapel itself is octagonal and centrally focussed like the earlier *Vidovdan Temple* and the later memorial chapel he built for his own family. The main sculptures are the *Virgin and Child*, *Crucifixion*, *St. Roch* and *Angels* bearing away the souls of the departed. The beauty of this monument lies in its clean stone lines and monumental appearance, both inside and outside and its lovely position on the Adriatic coast. It also however shows Meštrović's weaker sides as a builder: architecture conceived as sculpture — volume and surface and not composition in the approach to spacial dimensions. The interior is hardly more than an exhibition place for sculptures which have too little interrelationship. There is better harmony of architectural and sculptural elements on the facade of the building although here too the two caryatids only appear to bear the architrave, which has too small a pediment above it.

Basically similar in conception, but much better architecturally, is the sculptor's own family *Otavice Memorial Chapel* (1927—31). It is free of all external decorative reliefs, and makes its effect primarily by the impact of its clean stone dome. It dominates the whole naked landscape and is an impressive monument.

Another work on the borderlines between sculpture and architecture is the Unknown Soldiers' Tomb at *Avala* near Belgrade (1934—38). Basically it is a mausoleum with an emptiness that makes an unnatural effect, and caryatids that are unfunctional since they do not hold anything up. The approach to it has a northern formality and stiffness. Nevertheless the visitor cannot escape the suggestive monumentality of the tomb. Its outstanding position, the restraint of shape and decoration, the strength and nobility of the Jablanica granite of which it is built, all contribute to the effect of solemnity which such monuments seek to achieve. The granite caryatids seen from near make an even more striking effect. More functional, and architecturally more harmonious, are two similar caryatids in the sculptor's fireplace in his Split villa.

Among other buildings which Meštrović designed may be mentioned the *Art Gallery* in Zagreb (today the Museum of the People's Revolution) and the *King Zvonimir Chapel* in Biskupija near Knin. The first has a certain simplicity of form and material, and a monumentality which fits well into the part of the town where it is situated. But it proved unfunctional as an exhibition place because of the monotonous circle of the walls. The second was based on a similar church in the period of the medieval Croatian state and was considerably damaged during the war.

The *Meštrović Palace* in Split (1931—39), now the *Meštrović Gallery* is the most attractive of his buildings not so much because of any originality in its fairly conventional design, but because of its position and the splendid white stone from the Island of Brač of which it is built. There are impressive entrance steps leading to a porch with classical pillars, and through the pines and cypress at the edge of the garden the blue Mediterranean sea can be seen. One of the most representative collections of Meštrović's work is exhibited in the building and the surrounding garden.

Even more beautifully placed is Meštrović's *Kaštelet* (1937—39) not far from the gallery. This was a free adaptation of an old baroque fortified manor. Meštrović added a cloister courtyard and a chapel with wood carvings. This *Chapel of the Cross* is a special experience. In it Meštrović placed his huge *Crucifixion* (1917) and lined the walls with a whole series of carved panels of walnut wood showing *Scenes from the Life of Christ,* done over almost four decades (1917—1953). The greatest value of these is in their total effect, since in artistic quality they are very unequal. The finest and the most sculptural are the early *Jesus and the Woman* of *Samaria* and the *Annunciation*.

The last panels were almost conceived as graphic works. Not only in time but in artistic style the range is very great, but the chapel is unique, and the experience of the whole makes a deep effect.

∎

Ivan Meštrović was in Split when the Italian facists occupied the town in 1941. They had not forgotten his successful work for the liberation of Dalmatia during the First World War, and he was among outstanding personalities on their list for deportation and prison camp. Giovanni Papini warned him and he fled to Zagreb.

There, under the protection of Hitler's and Mussolini's troops, was created the Independent State of Croatia. The rulers of this new state tried to get Meštrović's support, counting on his reputation both at home and abroad. But even though he was offered a high position he could not agree with the regime. He could not forgive the giving of Dalmatia to the Italians, and especially he could not tolerate the persecution of those of Orthodox faith in Croatia, which reached terrible proportions. He decided to emigrate to England but his plan was discovered and he was put in prison. For four and a half months he was in prison, ill treated and sick, along with his friend Jozo Kljaković, waiting for a death sentence. He was pardoned at the last moment, after foreign intervention particularly on the part of the Vatican. He was then held in prison.

In his cell in Sava Street, Zagreb, from where hundreds were deported daily for execution and mass torture, Meštrović experienced the psychologically most terrible and most dramatic moments of his life, moments which were to leave indelible marks on his later work. These were far more immediate experiences than the generalized pessimism that he had felt during the First World War, when he had lived in comfort and freedom. It was now that he wrote his *Imaginary Conversations with Michelangelo,* and on packing paper drew sketches, of biblical subjects, among them several variants for a large *Pieta,* which some years later he was to complete in Rome. All his disappointment and bitterness, came to a head here added to a sense of helplessness and desertion as he waited for death in prison. And these personal feelings were sharpened by the knowledge that outside his cell there was an even greater prison, and that the whole world was in a frenzy of fratricidal destruction. Such feelings came to expression later in *Job,* one of Meštrović's most shattering works.

Accompanying his sculptures to the Venice Biennale in 1942 Meštrović emigrated to Rome and took refuge in the Croatian Society of St. Jerome. He made three reliefs for a new building they were putting up: *St. Jerome, Pope Sisto V* and *Pope Leo XIII*. And here, in a hired studio on the Pincio he modelled his *Rome Pieta.*

After this he escaped with his family to Switzerland, living first in Lausanne and later in Geneva (1943—46). He carved in wood and painted in oils. In Switzerland his book was published *Dennoch will ich hoffen* (Still We Will Not Give In), reflective dialogues written in Split on the eve of war. A study of Michelangelo, written in 1926, was published in 1943 in the Italian periodical *Parallelo*. The previously mentioned dialogues with Michelangelo did not come out until 1955—58 in a German translation in the periodical *Kunst ins Volk*. His last year in Switzerland Meštrović was seriously ill.

In 1946 he visited Rome once more for a short time and finished his big *Pieta*. Then the American Academy invited him to New York to arrange an exhibition of his works.

Living and working in Rome in 1942, and again in 1946, Meštrović once more came into contact with the works of Michelangelo. He had always admired the great Renaissance artist and had taken him as an example. Even in their lives the two sculptors had mainy points in common. At this particular moment Michelangelo's realistic sculpture had a particularly beneficial effect on Meštrović who seemed to be turning to almost graphic stylization, simplified forms, and metaphysical idealization. He now once more returned to vigorous and purely sculptural expression and regained the feeling for form and realism which had once been his great strength.

The work which for a number of years most occupied his energy and imagination, and in which he expressed the whole of his being, conscious that he was creating his life's masterpiece was his *Rome Pieta* (1942; South Bend, U. S. A.). This big marble group of four figures, composed in a pyramid form is complete and satisfying. There is a Laokoon-like restlessness of line, verticals, diagonals and horizontals which resolve themselves with the inevitable harmony of a fugue. The composition of this complex group, with the wonderfully moving position of the prone Christ, shows all the true sculptural qualities which were latent in Meštrović and which Michelangelo again called forth.

In the Rome reliefs of *St. Jerome* and *Pope Sisto V* (1942; Rome) Michelangelo's fertilizing influence is also apparent. Stylization is no more that of the graphic artist it is based on sculptural elements. A forceful power and energy radiates from these figures, both through facial expression and the whole composition. There is nothing superfluous or inessential in these reliefs. In 1945 in Switzerland Meštrović did about ten paintings in oils on religious subjects. These are basically sketches for sculpture without any particular artistic qualities in their own right, and especially not in use of colour. Here too Meštrović may be compared to Michelangelo who in most of his painting remained primarily a sculptor. Most of the subjects were far better done by Meštrović in sculptures. For example the big picture *The Last Supper* is in a wooden relief in the *Kaštelet*. The figure of Job in *Job's Arguments* is better done in stone and the same is true of *St. Jerome*.

Meštrović's many drawings from various periods are a special problem in any consideration of the whole of his work. They are never drawings in their own right. They are not vivid pencil improvisations as are Rodin's drawings, but almost always plans and projects for sculpture. But it is just in this that their special value and originality lie. For in most cases they are complete works, completely experienced and created. Their further implementation was usually a technical matter of transferring them to clay, plaster, stone, bronze or wood. Looked at from this point of view many of these drawings are of greater worth than the sculptures done from them.

After the war Ivan Meštrović decided to live in the United States. The University of Syracuse, New York State, hearing of his decision from the famous American sculptress, Malvina Hoffman, offered him the position of professor in their School of Art.

In 1947 the Metropolitan Museum in New York organized an exhibition of Meštrović's work, the first one-man exhibition by a living artist ever held there, under the patronage of the American Academy of Art and Letters. In the centre stood his great *Rome Pieta* "which", as a critic wrote, "seemed created to bring home to the American people who had not experienced war what had been happening in the world: the suffering and distress of the whole of deserted mankind..."

But although his work had been well known to the American pre-war public, since he had had so many exhibitions there, and been popular in cultural and political circles, for the new generation his work was foreign and old-fashioned. New art currents were coming to expression especially in America. Abstract art was dominant. Meštrović in his sculpture wished to propagate humanism and love. Official criticism praised him and acknowledged the special ethical message of his work. "In the Metropolitan exhibition is presented an artist and a humanist, able to express himself simply and directly in stone, wood and bronze."

But the old sculptor felt that time had overtaken him, and that he could no longer keep up with present day styles. Brancusi and Moore were the acknowledged great sculptors of the post-war world. In spite of everything he went on in his own way — not wishing and not being able to do otherwise. His misfortune was — as he used to say in joke — that he had not died earlier, but he was happy that he had not, because he still had much to give.

Meštrović's studio in Syracuse became a cultural centre of that university and the whole region. Drawn by his fame and thanks to his well known hospitality he was not only visited by acquaintances and friends but by people from all over America. The chair of sculpture was created especially for him, and was intended as a finishing school for seniors and postgraduates. One critic in *News Week* wrote: "The art that comes from Syracuse, whether or not its forms suit American taste, will certainly not be able to be ignored..."

Even so his fame in America remained a local, regional affair and was not national. America could not offer him the inspiration or the recognition that his own country had. For this reason he wanted his art to remain in his homeland. In 1912 he donated to the nation almost all the sculptures which were in it, and also his villa and *Kaštelet* in Split, and his house and studio in Zagreb, to be galleries for his work. He also left the family memorial chapel in Otavice as a national monument. In 1954 he finished his cycle of wood carvings of the *Life of Christ* to complete the interior of the Holy Cross church in *Kaštelet*. It was as if he thus fulfilled some promise made when he began to work on them almost 40 years earlier.

Although physically present in the New World Meštrović in fact continued to live in his homeland. The American way of life, contemporary events and even contemporary art could not interest him, he could find no basis for personal experience in them. He liked best, in the circle of his family or friends, to talk of old times or recite national poetry, which he remembered excellently from his childhood.

The famous American sculptress Malvina Hoffman did a fine bronze of Meštrović after his removal to America, and wrote a short study of his work in a New York periodical.

On his 75 birthday the University of Syracuse held an exhibition of his works and published two monographs *The Sculpture of Ivan Meštrović,* with an introduction by Norman Rice, and *Ivan Meštrović, Sculptor and Patriot,* with a biography by the Director of the Syracuse School of Art, Laurence Schmeckebier. The university also published a portfolio of his *Life of Christ* wood carvings.

In 1955 Meštrović went as professor of sculpture to Notre Dame University, South Bend, Indiana, where he lived and worked for the rest of his life. At that famous Catholic university he did much to develop religious sculpture in America which was then far behind that in Europe.

Although he represented an older generation, and had no effect on the development of contemporary style, the Americans knew how to value his general contribution to the new country in which he lived and worked. He was among 22 famous men on whom President Eisenhower personally conferred American citizenship in a White House ceremony in 1954. Many honours given to him also show the high regard which he enjoyed in artistic and academic circles. In 1948 he was given an honorary doctorate at Colgate University, and Ohio Wesleyan University. In 1953 The Academy of Arts and Letters in New York gave him an award. In 1955 he was presented with the American Institute of Architects' Medal for outstanding work on architectural decoration. He was also given honorary doctorates by Marquette University and Notre Dame. In 1956 he became honorary doctor of Columbia University. In 1960 he was elected member of the American Academy of Arts and Letters, in which the total number is limited to fifty. Since 1947 he had been a member of the Academy Institute for Arts and Latters, with 250 members.

Europe was equally proud of him. In 1952 he was elected honorary member of the Vienna Art Academy, and on the occasion of the 70 birthday the Academy organized an exhibition and placed his bronze *Selfportrait* in the atrium of their building.

Meštrović's working energy did not slacken to the end. Misfortune, life abroad, age, family tragedies, illness none of these could affect his creative energy. ''The only way to be an artist is to work. I am used to it. My pupils want to work two or three hours a day. They will never achieve anything that way'' he said in an interview in March 1962. Only a few weeks later he died.

In the sixteen years that he lived and worked in America, already an old man, he made almost a hundred works large and small. These do not in the least show any signs of age and tiredness in manner or in repetition of subject indeed many of them give out a feeling of new, almost of youthful freshness. But there are great differences in quality and style. In the church pieces and portraits of people done to commission there is a measure of monotony, uninventiveness and routine. This is not so in the works he created freely.

On one hand he continued to use elements of decorative stylization, but on the other he almost returned to his impressionist period in modelling. This also meant a return to the more realistic, to the intimate, lyrical or dramatic realization of the anatomy of the naked human body. Is *Happy Youth* (1946; South Bend, Split), the delicate figure of a girl in movement, a personification of a longing for youth, or of disappointment in so many ideals? Or is it a return to the beginning, a closing of the circle?

Most of his sculptures while he was in America were religious. The reason for this is that the Church was his main patron. He was very highly thought of and much in demand in church circles in America, not only because he taught at a Catholic university, but because the Church found it very difficult to adopt to the works of contemporary, mainly non-figurative, sculptors. It needed its message to be clear and unmistakable and Meštrović's works were always a kind of spiritualized and humanistic realism. He had always been driven by the need to provide ethical more than esthetic work. Even during the First World War, after his exhibition at Leeds, the rector of that university, Sadler, had with great foresight said: ''In you we have the greatest religious sculptor since the Renaissance.''

But Meštrović's religious feelings were not dogmatic and narrow, as they are sometimes presented. It was the Bible that was his inspiration, not the catechism. In the figures of the Bible, whether those of the prophets or of Christ, he saw and gave substance to personifications of goodress, truth, faith, suffering, and hope just as he had once done in the heroes of Kossovo or in his classical statues. It is interesting that in his own country, we know from a letter to a friend, a translation of the Koran was always on his desk, and that he loved to read it. We can see this universal element too in the greatest work that he projected, and unfortunately did not finish, during his stay in America the *Monument to the Jewish Martyrs* (1952). That same Christian *Moses* (1915, 1926, 1953) to which Meštrović kept returning under the unforgettable impact of Michelangelo's *Moses* now symbolically became the accuser on behalf of six million slaughtered Jews. Essentially for Meštrović, the man was always more important than his faith, and faith itself more important than the confession of it. This makes it possible to understand his sculptures of the Egyptian Gods *Isis and Horus* (1947; South Bend) done with the same piety, even with the same stylization as many of his sculptures of the *Madonna and Child.*

We need to understand this before we can take in to the full what was perhaps the greatest work that he ever did in America, and one of his finest works of any period, *Job* (Syracuse, Split). This naked, suffering, crouching form is in line with Rodin's understanding of sculpture. Indeed it has some formal, but in no way essential, familarities with Rodin's *Woman Crouching* which in sculptural qualities is far behind *Job.*

The first idea for *Job,* and for his companion piece *Jerolim* (1954; Washington), was born in Meštrović's prison cell in 1941. It was here that he reached the depths of his pain and disappointment in suffering mankind. Surrounded by cries that woke neither pity nor help a feeling of utter desolation was born with earth far away and heaven deaf, as in Job's own words "Behold I cry out of wrong, but I am not heard: I cry aloud, but there is no judgment" (Job, 19:7).

The figure made a great impression at Meštrović's New York exhibition in 1947. One critic, Carlyle Burrows, wrote; "Most impressive of all is the figure of *Job* into which he has poured a concentration of emotion greater than into any other work. This realistic figure gives an incredible impression of spiritual and physical suffering." *Job* was Meštrović's last truly great work, on a level with his *Kraljević Marko, Crucifixion, Psyche* and his American *Indians.*

At the opposite pole from Job's despair stands the quiet concentration of *St. Jerome* in the park of the College of the Croatian Franciscans in New York. *Job's* protest is made to the outside world; *Jerome's* meditations are inturning.

Among the many figures he made to go in churches particularly noteworthy are the bronze statue of *John the Baptist* (1954) in the baptistry of Split cathedral, which was once the Roman Temple of Mars. The ascetic figure of this saint, his extended arms, and the expression on his face, give an overall feeling of tranquillity achieved through suffering. John the Baptist fits far better into his classical surroundings than *Bishop Gregory of Nin* did when he stood in the Peristyle. An unusually lyrical work, more than simply a work of faith, is his *Jacob's Well* (1957). These free standing figures in the park of the University at South Bend are linked by the pure geometry of the well head. There are similarities here with the bas-relief carving of Christ and the *Woman of Samaria* in *Kaštelet,* which though it has less sculptural power has more poetry. This work by Meštrović is nearest to contemporary style.

The bronze *Persephone* (1946; Syracuse and Split) and *Atlantide* (1946; South Bend; Split) also stand out among Meštrović's later work. These nudes are nearer to Rodin than to Bourdelle or even to Maillol. We can enjoy these figures purely as sculptures, without taking into account their titles and meaning, here too however Meštrović was giving expression to the tragedy and suffering, personified in Persephone, the daughter of Zeus, who Hades took to the underworld, and who cried out in vain as did Job. One of these bronze figures stands in the courtyard of the University of Syracuse, the other in the gardens of Meštrović's villa in Split. The figure of *Atlantide* is a soft spiral as if she were falling like a flower from a broken stem.

Blind Homer (1956; South Bend) is a later conception of the *Blind Fiddler* of the *Vidovdan Temple,* for man and his fate have essentially always been the same. The destruction of the sculptor's ideals and of those of so many other men is personified in *Icarus* (1947); South Bend) and The *Fall of Icarus* (1954; South Bend), free and contemporary sculptures.

It is natural to expect that Meštrović's nostalgia and love for his homeland would come to expression in his work and so it did in *Croaiian Rhapsody* (1947; Syracuse), which is among his spiritually most deeply felt and stylistically purest works. It has obvious similarities to the attractive seated *Girl with a Lute* (1927) in the Tate Gallery, London, but while the *Girl* is lyrically conceived the later sculpture is an embodiment of strength.

Just because of his unassuageable nostalgia for home Meštrović seldom refused a request to make sculptures, whether for public statues or for altars. Often his emotion was stronger than his artistic sense and all such works are not on the same level. His monument of

Juraj the Dalmatian for example that stands outside Juraj's great Šibenik Cathedral cannot be compared to the carvings of the Renaissance master. More successful is the intimate portrait of *Andrija Kačić Miošić* (1957), the writer Meštrović had so much loved when a boy in his village. This now stands in Kačić's birth place of Zaostrog in Dalmatia.

The last great memorial that Meštrović presented to his homeland was the huge statue of the Montenegrin poet *Petar Petrović Njegoš.* The project for a memorial chapel to the writer of *The Highland Wreath* (a poem written by Njegoš) to stand on Mount Lovćen was drawn up by Meštrović in 1932 and also a sketch for the monument, a seated figure with an open winged eagle above it. The sculpture was worked out in America, and carved on Jablanica granite in Meštrović's Split studio by his one-time pupil the sculptor Andrija Krstulović in 1958. Meštrović did not live to see the finish of this memorial chapel just as he had not lived to see so many of his other projects realized.

One more impressive statue, on a theme which Meštrović had returned to time and again, is *Mourning* (1958), in the centre of a monument that he made in Florida, and with this we may round off our short account of the rich creative work of Ivan Meštrović.

Meštrović lived the last years of his life in Indiana, working continually and always longing for his homeland.

On his seventieth birthday he spoke these warm and human words: "I remember my father and my grandfather, when they reached the age I have today used to say" "what is there to say of our years and our life?". Now the swift passing of time has brought me here too. I am not disturbed by the fact that my years are nearing their end, for ordinary physical existence is not so important, and man retains a certain feeling of duty. But sometimes I am disturbed by the questions: "What does our life mean as a whole? What have you achieved of all the things you dreamed of? What censure do you merit and in what surroundings for having done less than you wanted to?"

When we are forty we ask ourselves such questions for the first time, and I comforted myself then, that I still had time to perfect myself. When I was fifty these questions troubled me more. By the time I was sixty I realized that a man cannot move mountains, and now I am seventy I comfort myself thus: "Work while you still can, and as much as you can, until the end of your working days which are not far off."

Common sense tells me that I do not need to grieve about my fate. Other people just like me have passed through the same misfortunes. I cannot and I will not grieve about the world. The artist by his nature and calling is a foreigner, whether he lives in his own country or abroad, he must accept his fate and find his *chez soi* inside himself. But in my life one of my bitterest heritages has been poverty: the poverty of my family and of my nation. The first helped me never to fear material difficulties for I knew that I could never fall lower than I began. The second turned me inside myself to my work with the feeling that at last, within me, the poverty of my people would be lessened. Always deep within myself I heard a whisper "My country, so poor and small to the world, to my heart you are the greatest and the dearest." It was this that made it possible for me to finish some important works in my lifetime. It does not matter that life has carried this weak tree of my body into foreign countries, its roots always take strength from the small, infertile land in which they were first put down."

The American countryside could never take the place of his old varied and picturesque homeland. He would spend his summer holidays in the forests of Massachusetts on the shores of Connecticut and Long Island, but he was always inviting old friends to talk to them about his homeland. For the same reason he often visited New York, just to see if he could meet some fellow countrymen. "He would gather a number of us together", said an old friend, "and over a glass of wine and a cup of coffee tell of his life, never without a cigarette between his nicotine yellow fingers. He had wonderfully shaped hands, like a sculptor should.

When he talked his words flowed like a broad river in epic breadth. His voice was deep and monotonous, without variation . . . When he was at his best then he would quite spontaneously produced hundreds and hundreds of lines of national poetry . . . Through these poems he retained his link with his country and his people."

Unable to bear any longer his longing for home the old sculptor, in the summer of 1959, crossed the sea and for the last time in life visited his own country. There things had radically changed, he was impressed with the economic development of the country, but he found few old friends left. Milan Čurcin and Svetozar Rittig were old and ill in Zagreb, and the others were already dead. He went to Brioni as the guest of Marshal Tito. What gave him most satisfaction was his return to Split. It gave him particular pleasure, and a feeling of fulfilment, to find that his Split villa and the nearby *Kaštelet*, which he had presented to the nation, and also his Zagreb home, had been turned into exhibition galleries where his works lived on, seen by thousands of Yugoslav and foreign visitors every year. He went to his family memorial chapel in Otavice, and stayed in Drniš to open a little gallery of his works. He went back to America "spiritually and physically refreshed and strengthened."

A year before his death he had the pleasure of seeing his memoires published, *Memories of Political Men and Events*, which was in fact the confession of a famous political personality and artist who for half a century had been at the centre of many decisive events.

His life was nearing its end. But fate was unsparingly cruel to him in his last years. The first blow was the death of his daughter (1960) in the best years of her life. Then he had a stroke which partly affected his sight. Finally his son Tvrtko, the only one still in Yugoslavia, died tragically. This last was the bitterest blow of all, but he received the news of it, like all others, in silence, neither complaining nor bewailing. He poured out his sorrow in his last moving sculptures, *An Old Father in Despair at the Death of His Son* and *A Father Taking Leave of His Son in Fierce Embrace*. To this diptych he added *A Mother with Gentle Kiss Takes Leave of her Dead Daughter*. His last great triptych was finished.

But still he did not stop working. In the autumn of 1961 he did his last *Selfportrait*: a tired, sad old man, bent under the blows of life, but not broken. "I long ago vowed that I would work up to my last day," he said to his wife. And truly on the last day of his life he did go to his studio — but this time he was not to work. Death overcame him January 20, 1962, in South Bend, U. S. A. His body was taken back to his own country and buried in the family memorial at Otavice.

On the bell of the Cavtat Memorial Chapel, into which he had poured so much of his faith, he had engraved words that might have served for himself:

"Learn the secret of love and you will discover the secret of death and believe in life eternal!"

He lives on in his works.

The greatness and at the same time tragedy of Meštrović is that he was the typical Renaissance universal personality, and that he exhausted his powers in many fields. He wanted to go to the heart of everything, and go into every problem in all its complexity. As a sculptor he worked in stone, bronze and wood; he painted in oils and made drawings and frescoes; he was the arhitect of several buildings; he always had poetic ambitions hidden within him, left from the time of his youth when he had written national and religious poetry; he was a writer with a leaning towards the reflective; and finally he was active in the field of politics which took a great deal of his creative energy and his life, brought him eulogies and attacks, both of which meant lack of understanding and realization of his art. Such versatility might have been fully productive in classical times or in the Renaissance, but not in the specialized twentieth century world. It was one of the essential reasons that Meštrović's art was so uncontemporary. But when we consider independently the artistic and sculptural qualities of his huge opus, we still find enough first class works to fill whole galleries, enough for three productive lives. Many of the stormy ideas that moved Meštrović may well be forgotten, but his works will live on and they will show his art.

To find for his work, its style and ideas, its proper place is very difficult. His richness and variety were often achieved by opposing traits, which does not allow him to be fitted neatly into any art category. Is it possible to unite Secession and Rodin, Bourdelle and Maillol, Gothic and Classical, Egypt and Michelangelo? This is also Meštrović's tragedy, that the histories of art cannot find a proper place for him in their surveys of world art, and so they often leave him out.

Although we are not yet distanced enough from his work, nor do we have a fully comprehensive survey of sculptures which are scattered all over the world, nevertheless some conclusions are possible.

There is a basic duality, of completely opposed feeling, ideological and formal, running through his work from the very beginning. Is this rooted in some primaeval sense brought from his village, or was it acquired in his stormy life? Is it an expression of the duality of his people on the crossroads between past and future, on the borders of East and West? One thing that is certain is that from the beginning to the end we can trace the existence of two opposites: the monumental and the intimate. We can see the two in architecture. The former in his emotional and monumental *Vidovdan Temple* and *Unknown Soldier's Tomb* the latter in the southern intimacy warmth of his villa, and his *Kaštelet* in Split. The monumental expresses a longing for the symbolic. The intimate is pure sculptural form as in his marble nudes of women. In the one we have stillness and suffering, in the other music and joy. The former has affinities with the mystique of the East and finds affinities with Egypt, the Byzant the Middle Ages and the Slav past, while the other has its links with Mediterranean realism, and the sculpture of classical Greece, Renaissance Italy and the Roman components of cultural and art tradition.

If we compare Meštrović with his forerunners, or with those who started new styles, then he seems unimportant. For he was not a forerunner in his time nor was he the representative of a particular style. But he had inherited something that the *avant-garde* artists had never had: the mature synthesis of a whole rich past. Artists of this kind were never teachers and never had any special following. But if they were not representatives of a style, they were representatives of a time. Not Michelangelo, nor Goethe, nor Beethoven nor Tolstoy were as *avant-garde* as many of their lesser contemporaries. But their greatness lay in the fact that in them was expressed the complexity of a whole great period.

His style did not have an important influence on the further development of either Yugoslav or world sculpture, nor did he have many followers. But the force of his artistic personality, expressed in works in marble, bronze and wood, scattered in galleries and collections all over the world, gives Meštrović an outstanding place in the history of art not only of his own country, but of the world. Like no other single artist from his nation he grew beyond national frontiers and became an artist on the world level, part of the world's rich and universal cultural heritage.

Among his papers after his death the following note in his own hand was found:

''If we work only for this century we have little chance of lasting into the next. This century must be intended for all centuries.''

Duško Kečkemet

6

8

14

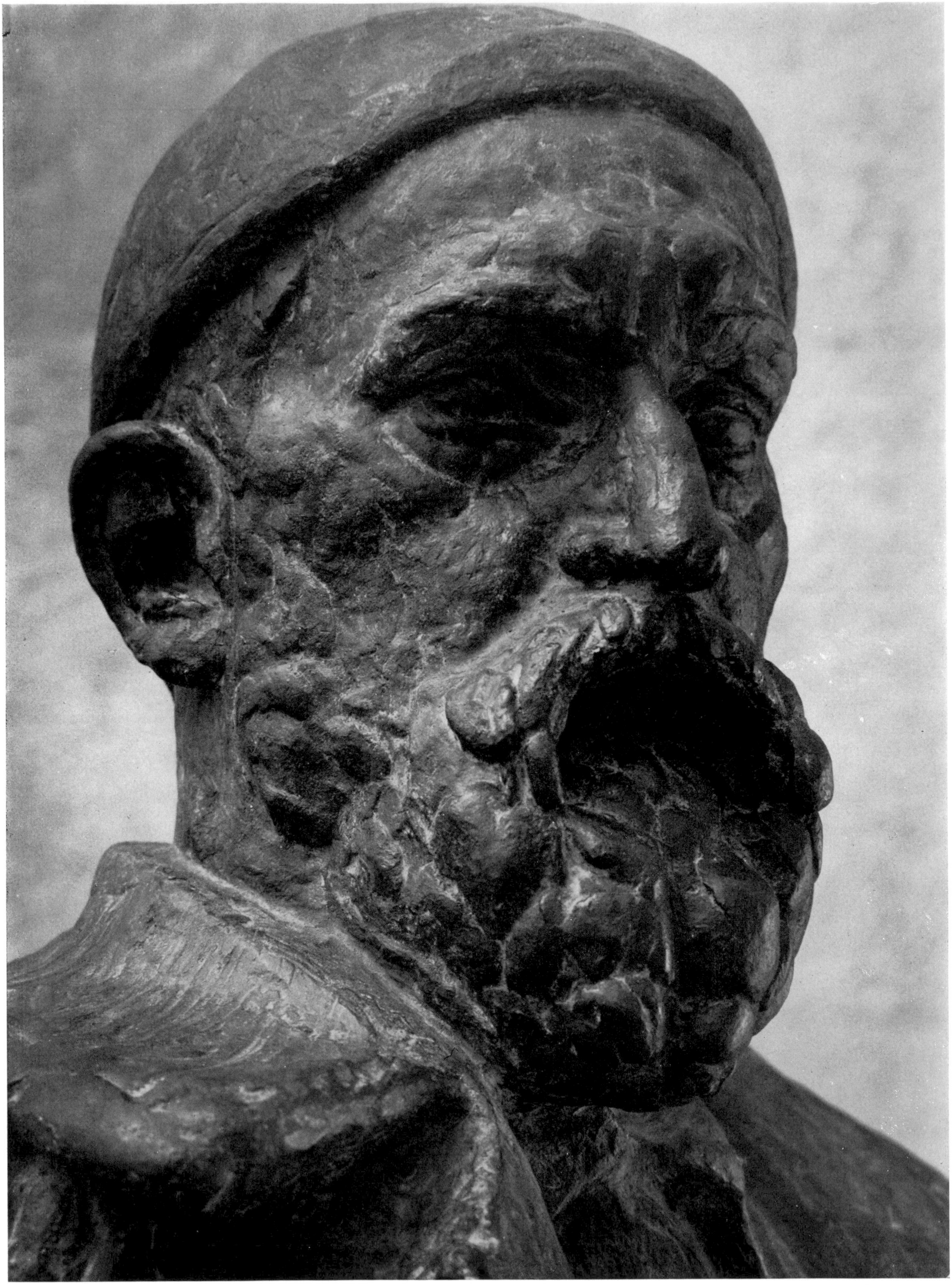

20

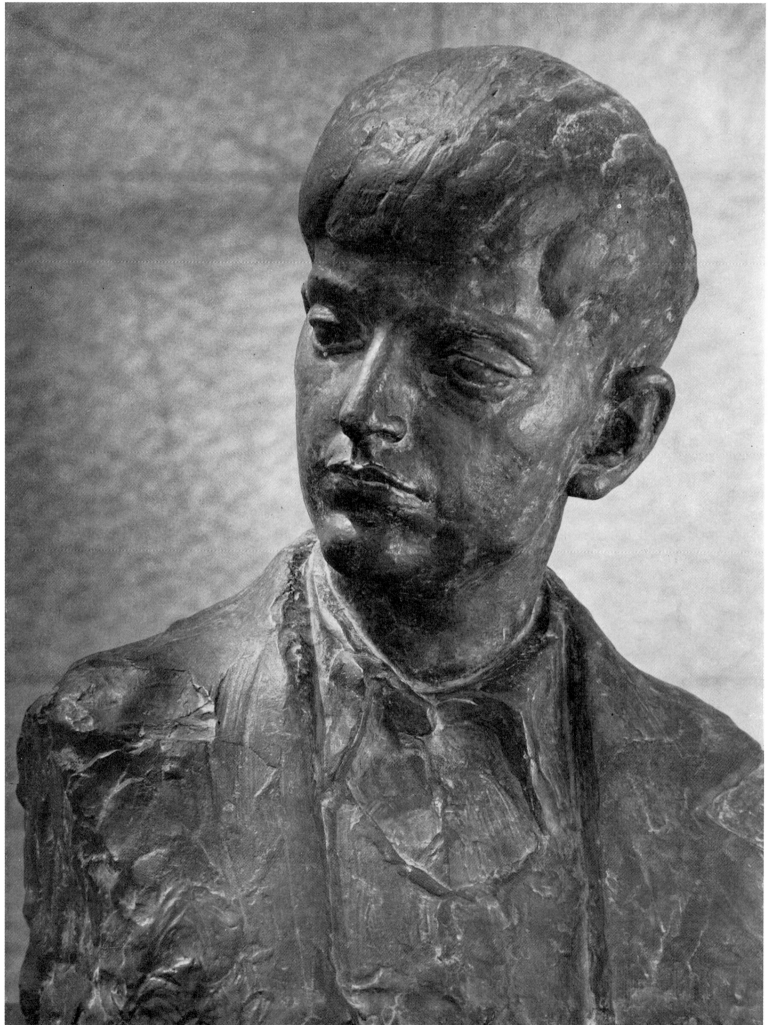

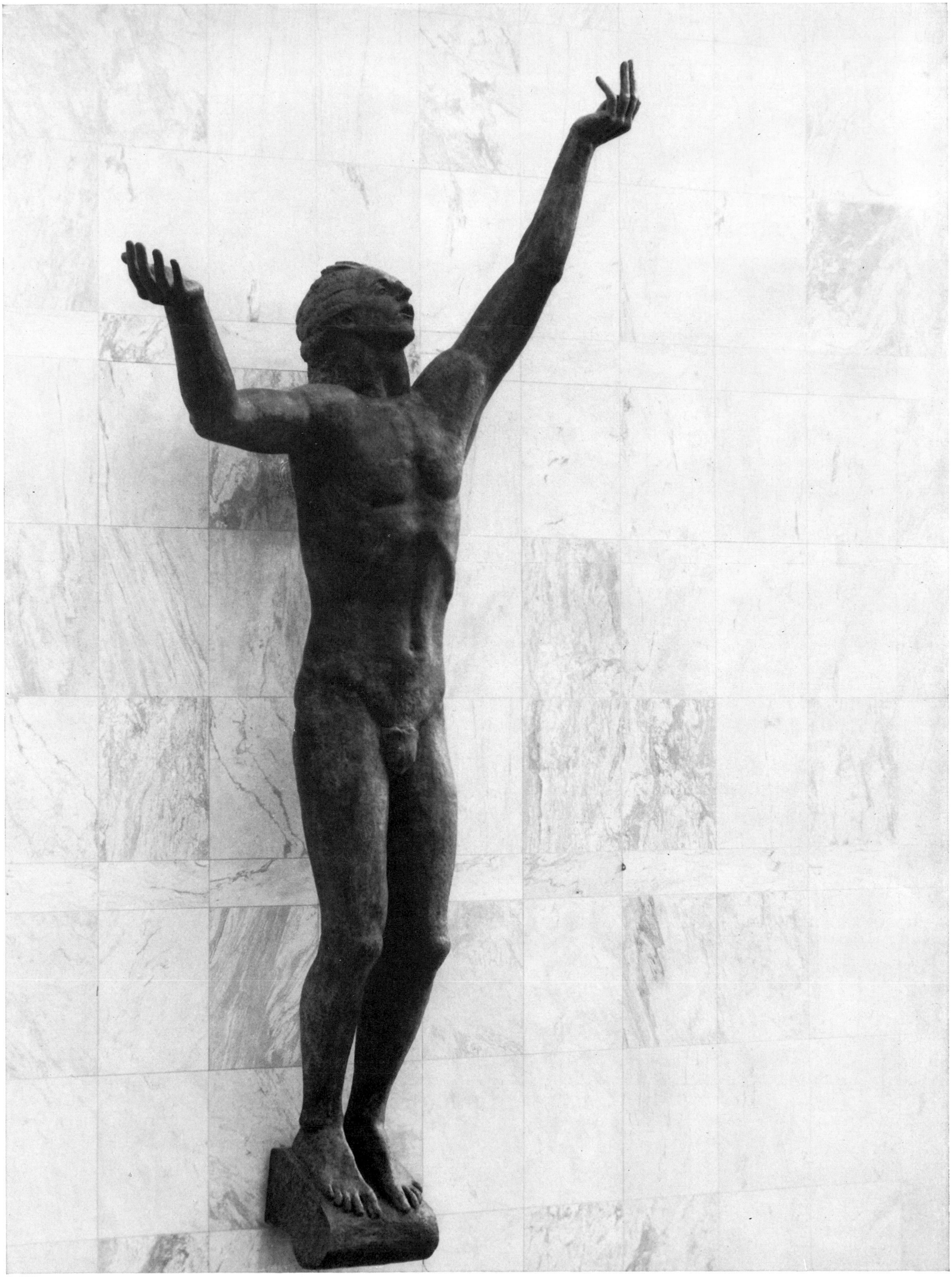

32

33

34

40

42

44

46

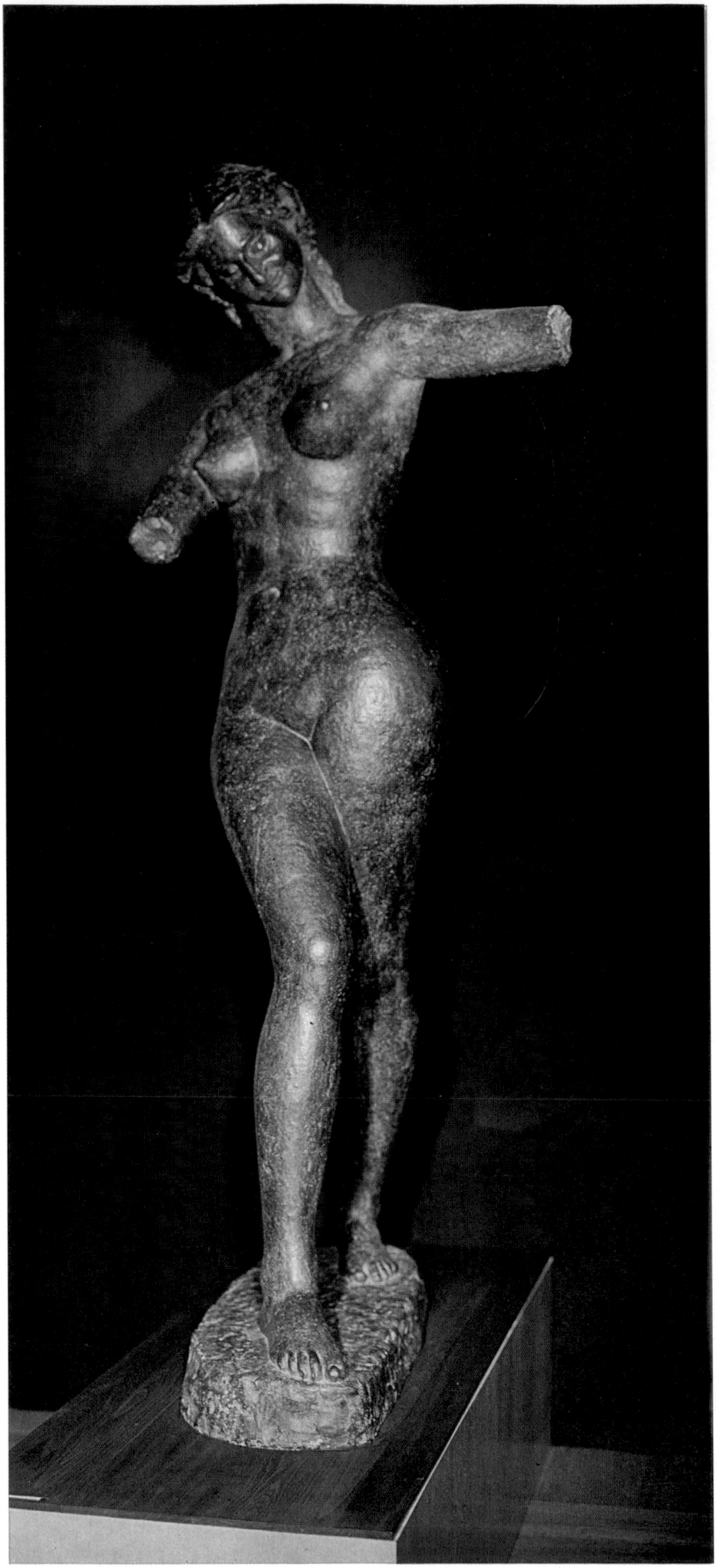

48

54

58

62

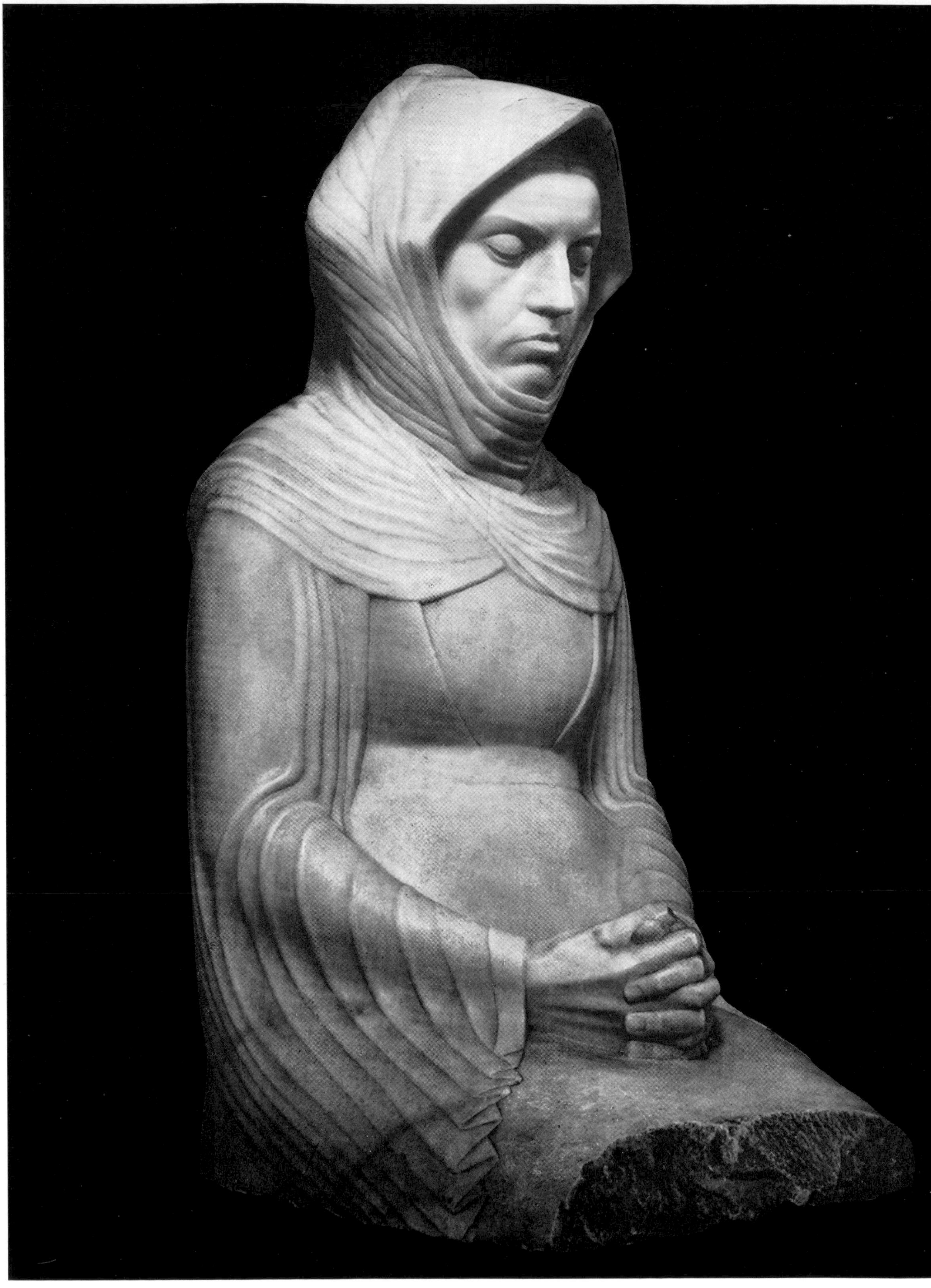

64

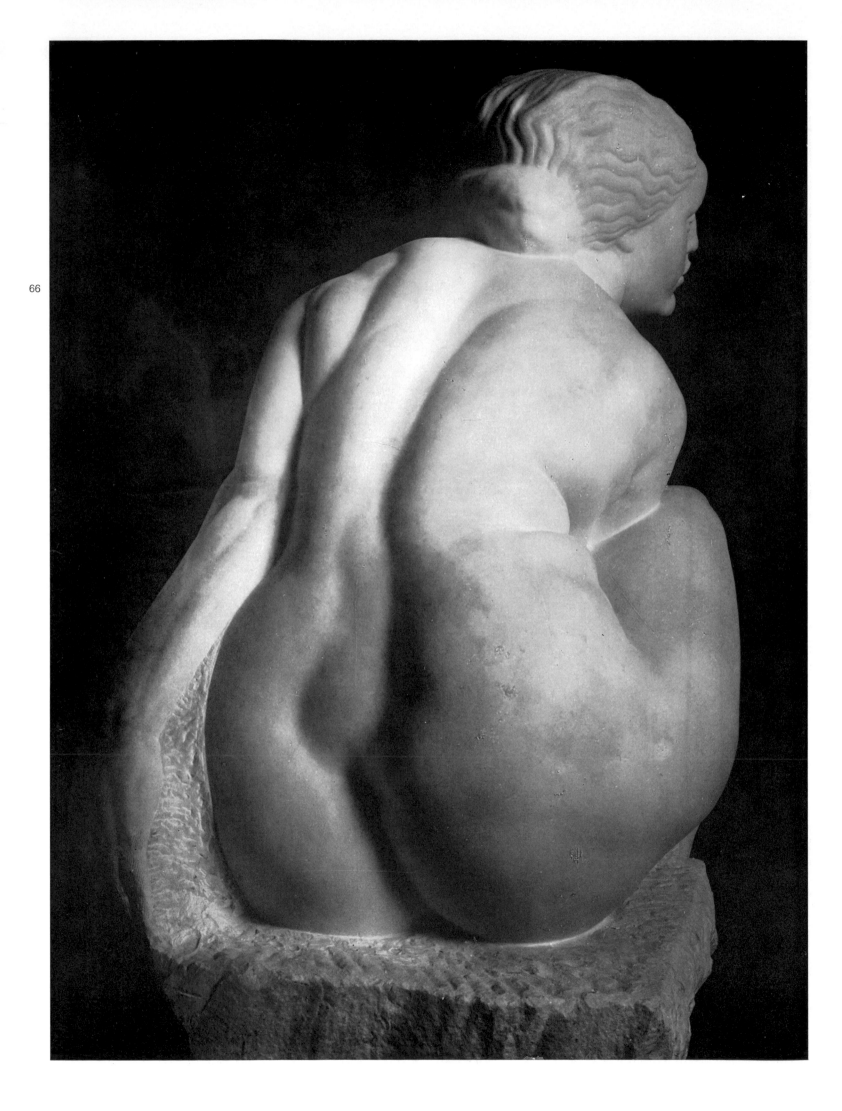

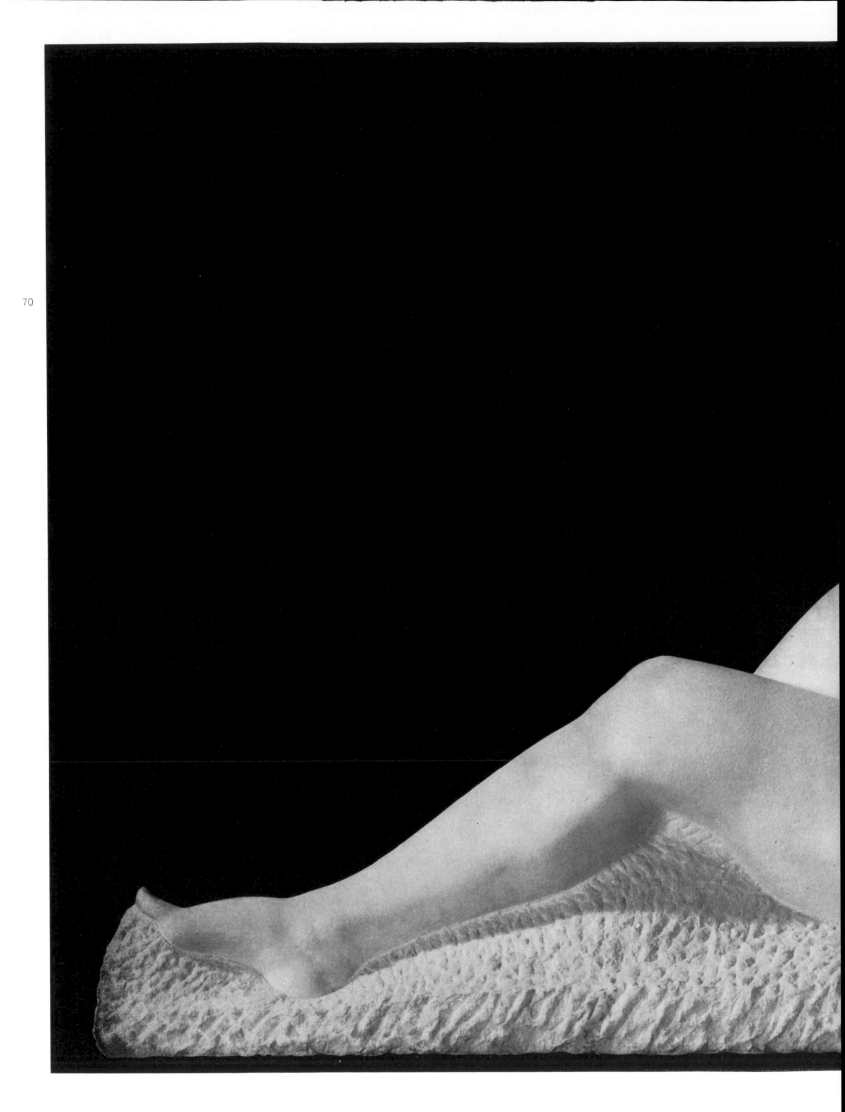

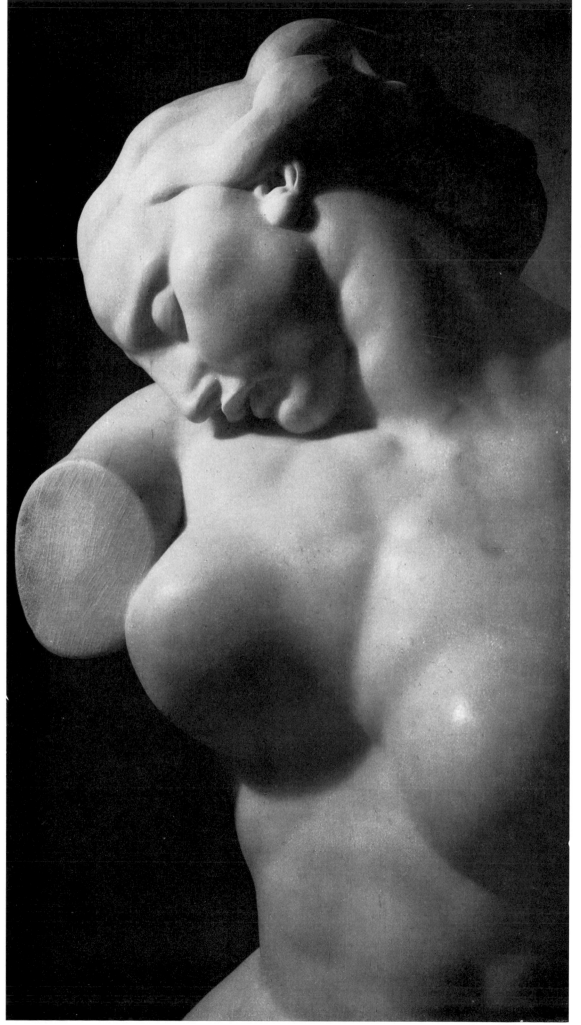

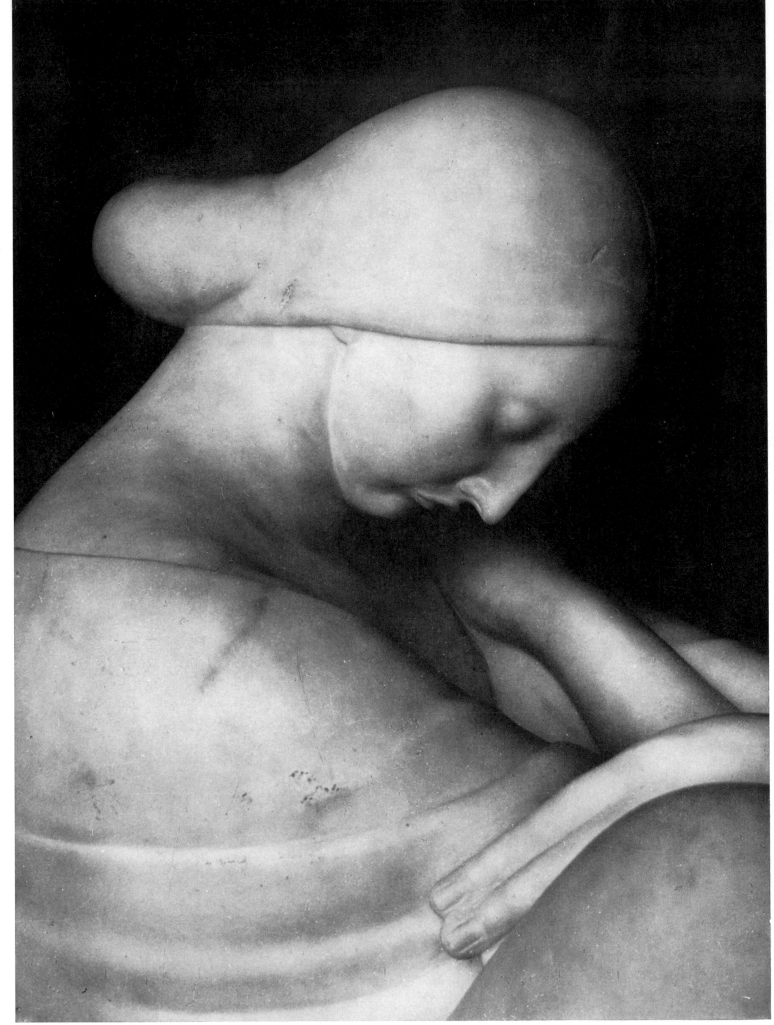

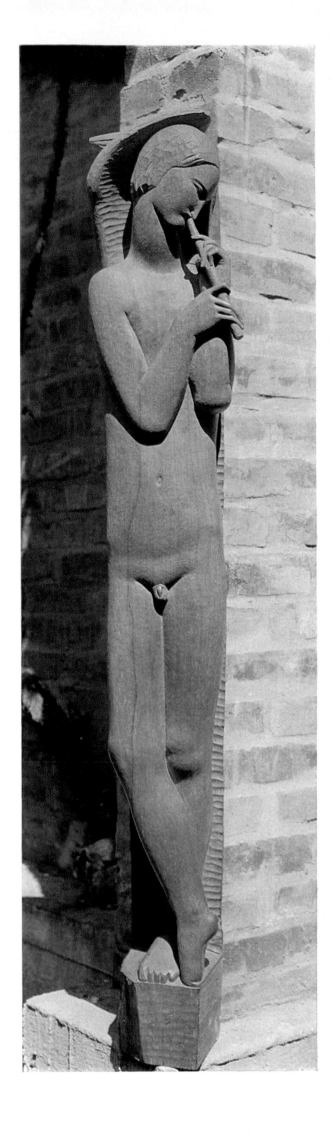

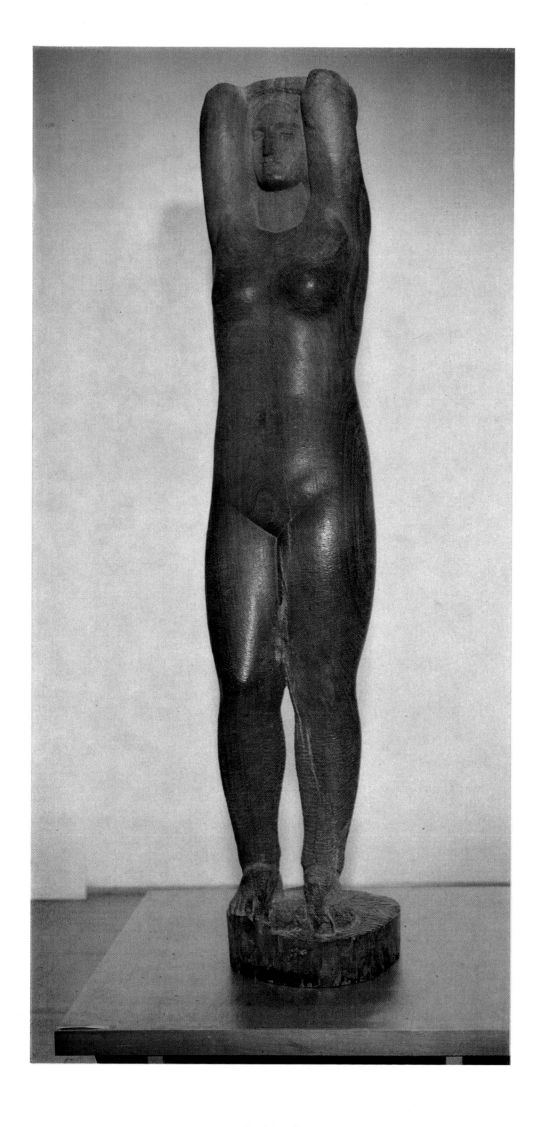

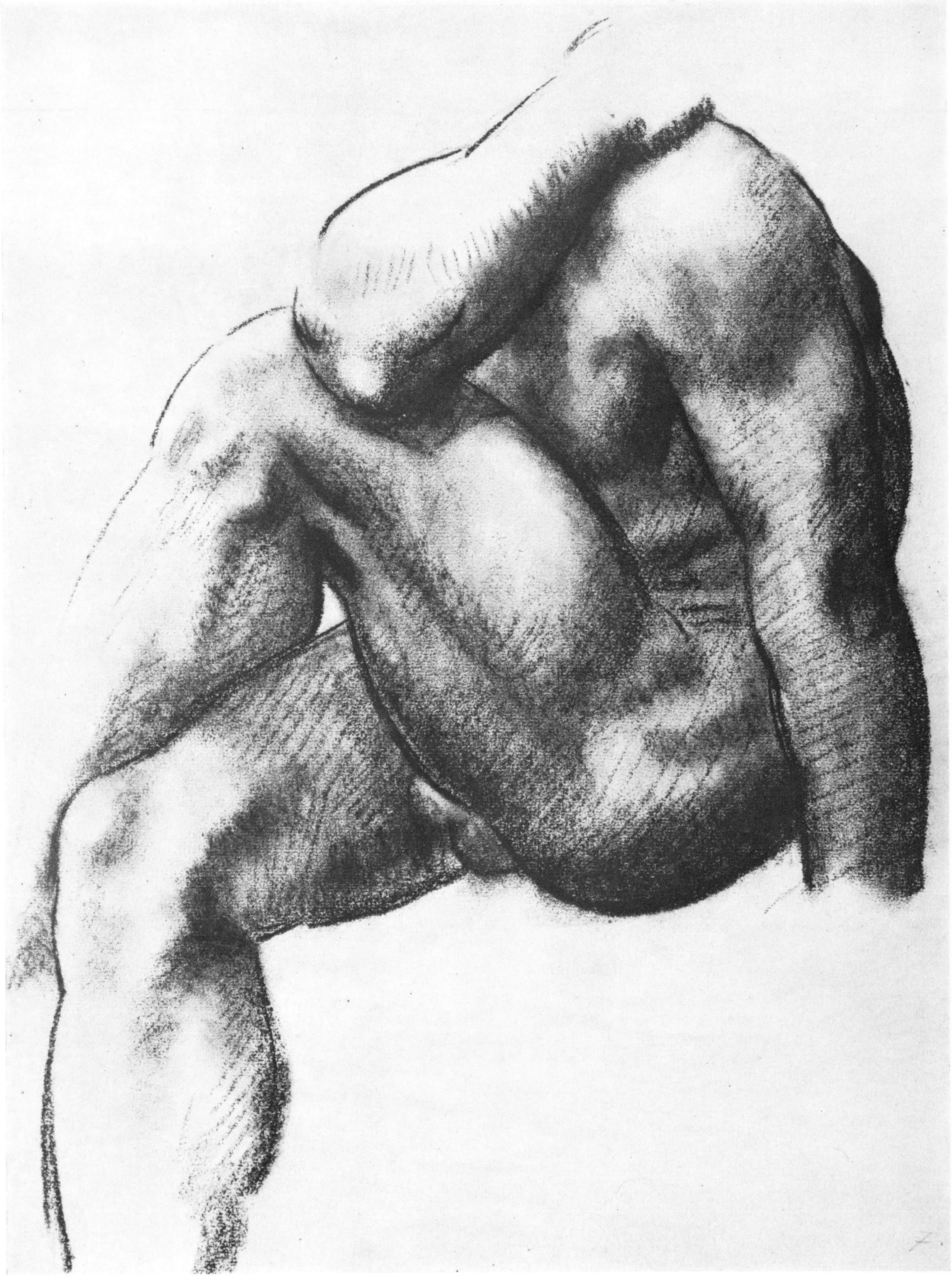

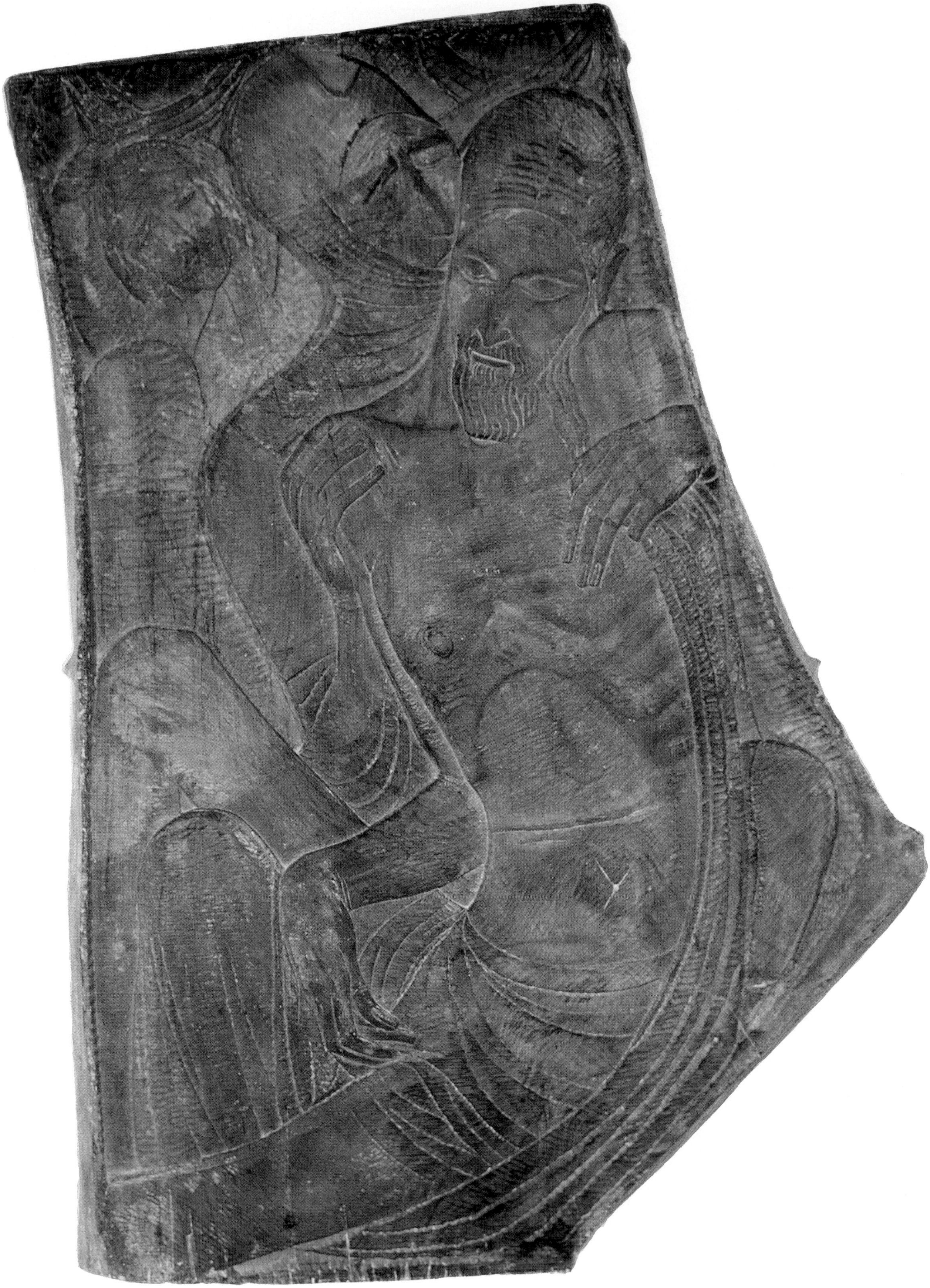

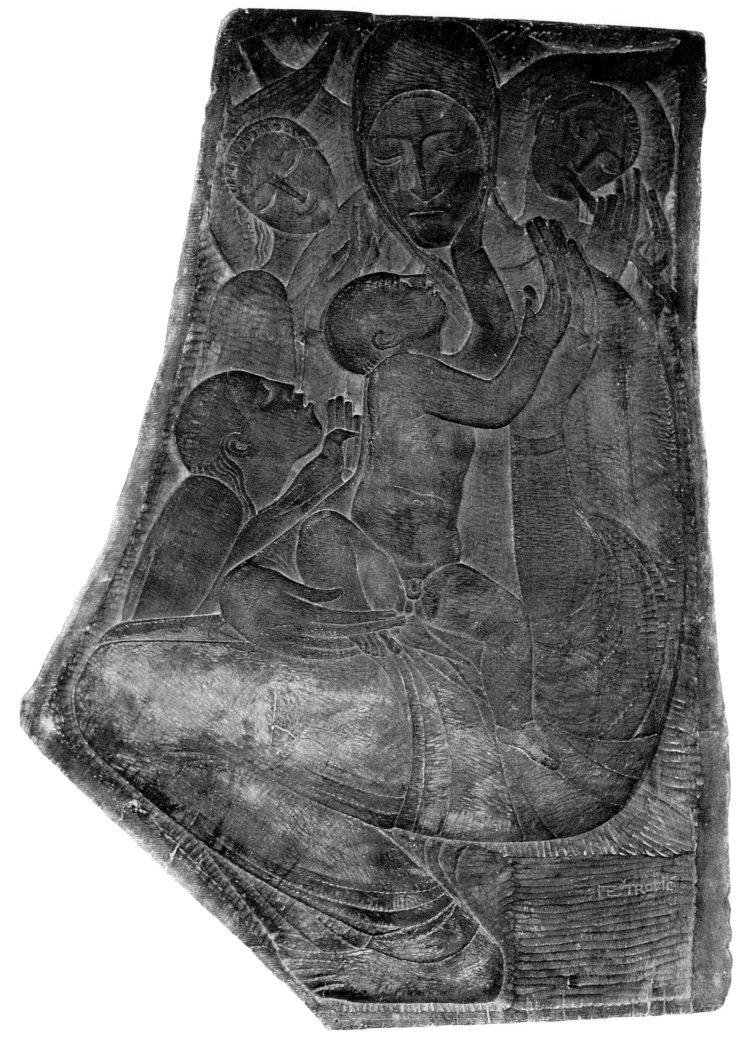

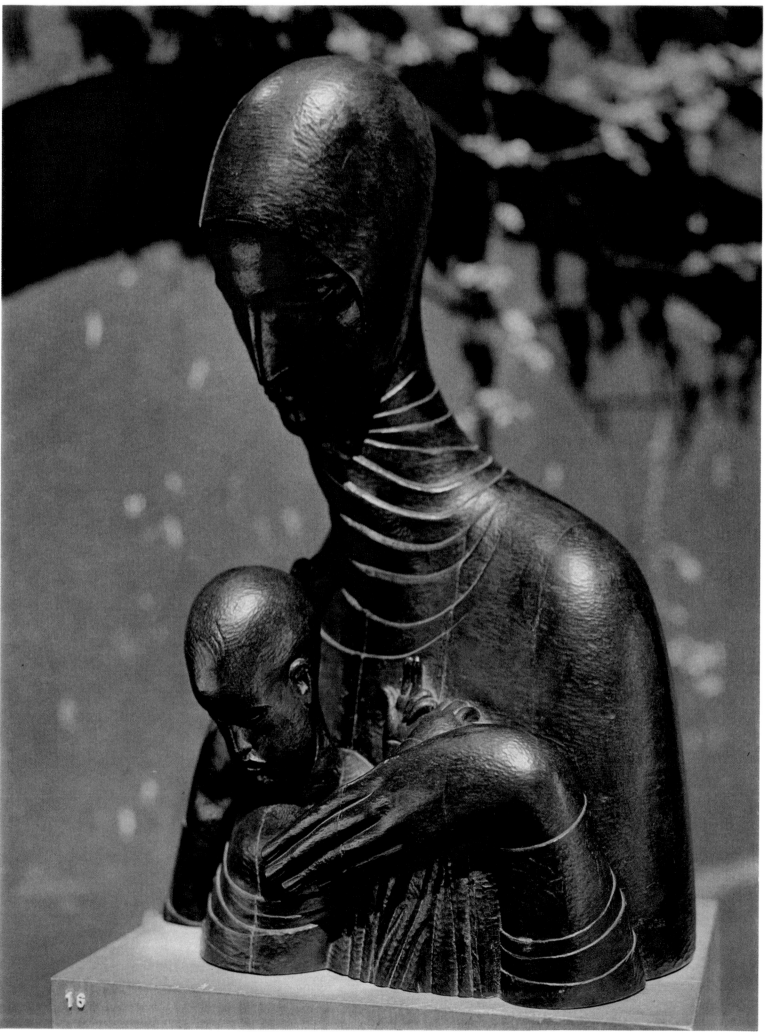

120

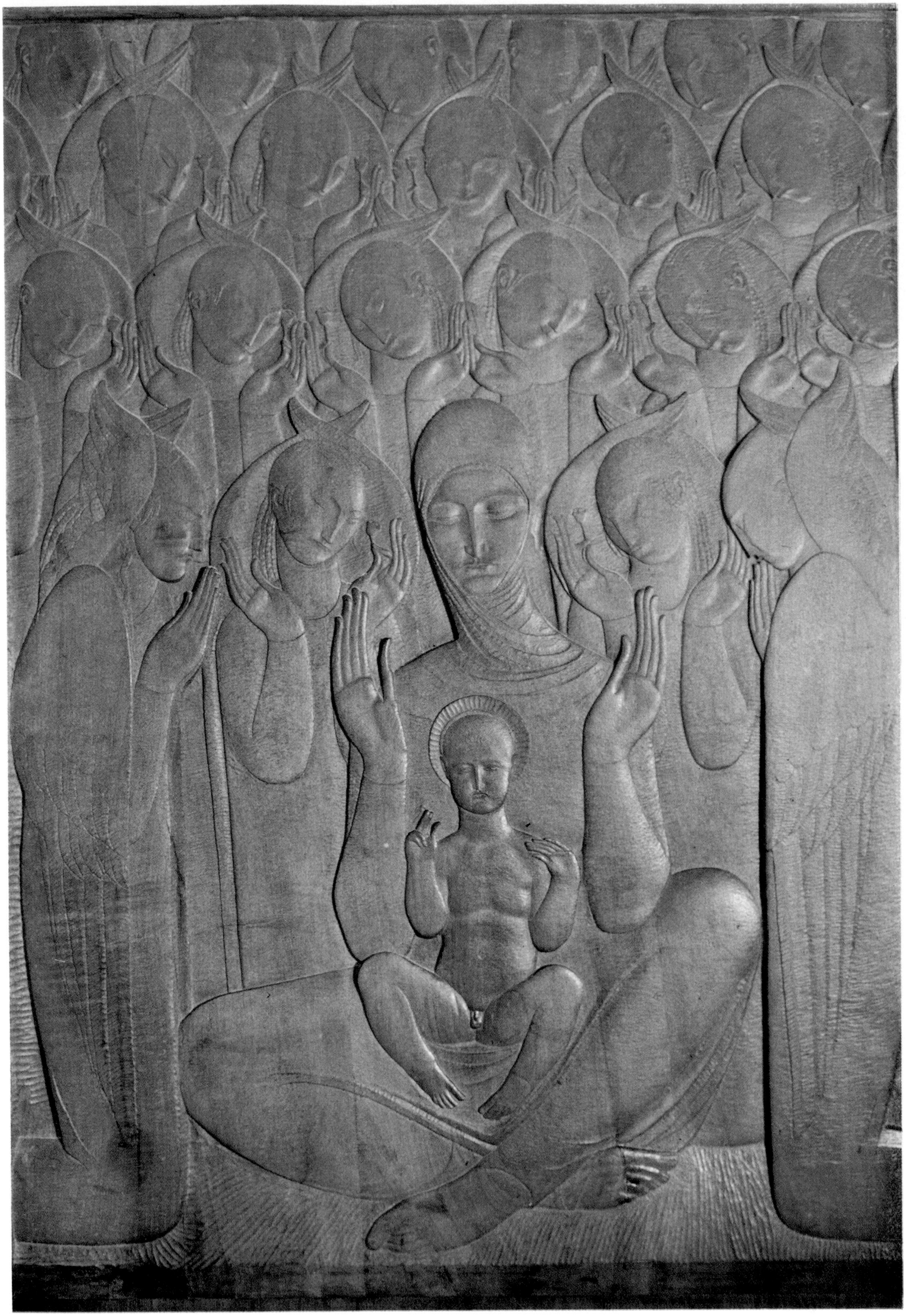

121

122

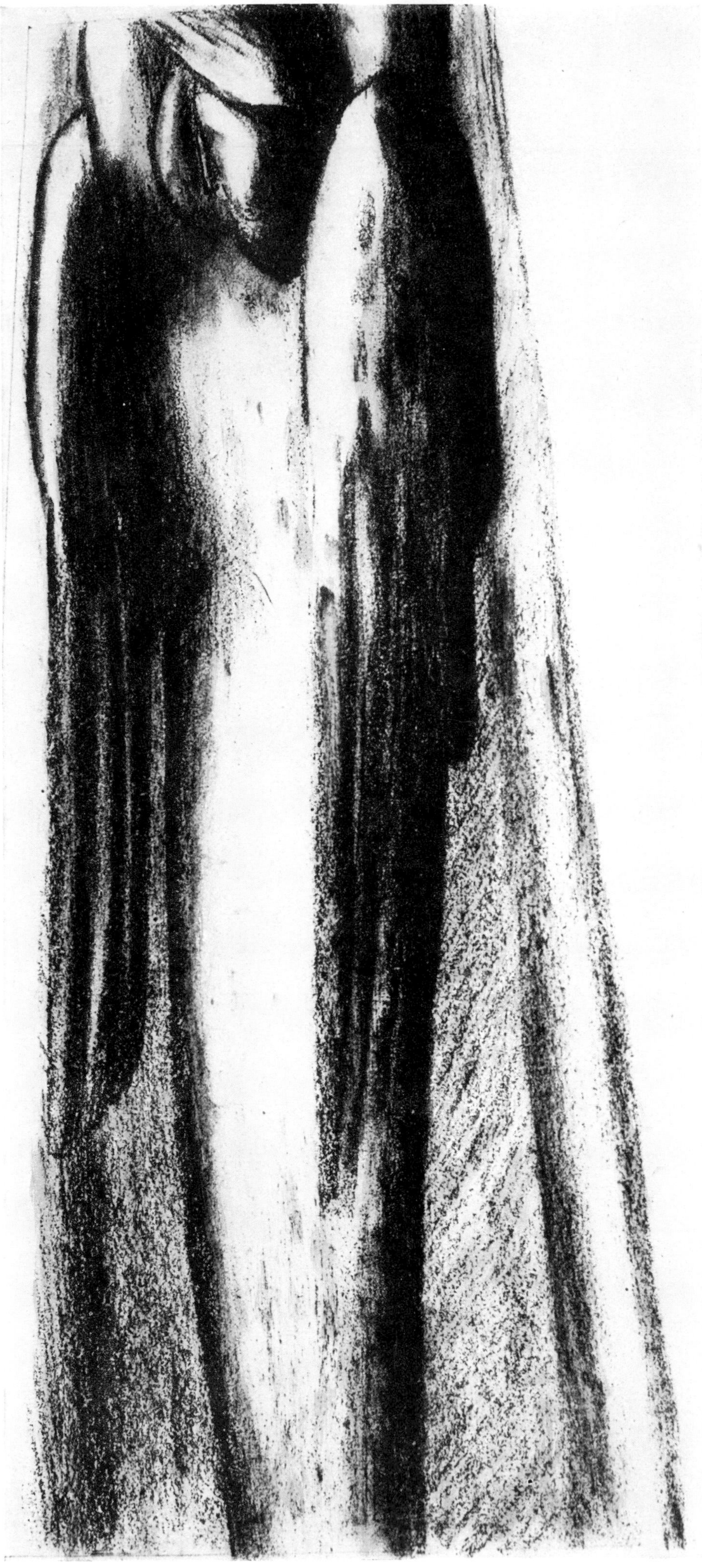

Extended review of works

Quotations

Bibliography

Catalogue of reproductions

Bosnian on Horseback, 1898
done when a boy, stone, 20 cm
Gallery of Art, Split

Izidor Kršnjavi, 1904
bronze, 92 cm
Meštrović Studio, Zagreb

Mother and Child
stone, 70 cm
National Museum, Budapest

Frieze of Warriors, 1909
marble, 90 cm, vase

My Mother, 1908
marble, detail
National Museum, Belgrade

Kossovo Maiden, 1907
marble
National Museum, Belgrade

My Father, 1910
bronze
National Museum, Belgrade

Vidovdan Temple, 1912
wood, model
National Museum, Belgrade

Srđa Zlopogleđa
bronze, head
National Museum, Belgrade

Caryatid, 1911
wood
National Museum, Belgrade

The Victor, 1913
monument
Kalemegdan Park, Belgrade

The Victor, 1913, bronze
figure on the monument
Kalemegdan Park, Belgrade

Head of the Victor, 1913
bronze, 37 cm
Meštrović Gallery, Split

Portrait of Mrs. H., 1914
bronze
Private Collection, Prague

Girl at prayer, 1915
plaster, 76 cm
Glyptotheca, Zagreb

Boy's Head, 1915
bronze, 30 cm
Meštrović Gallery, Split

Lamentation, 1915
plaster, 55×38 cm
Glyptotheca, Zagreb

Lady Ratcliffe, 1917
bronze
Private Collection, Leeds

Virgin and Child, 1917
wood
Artist's own Collection,
South Bend

Anđa Petrović
bronze, 61 cm
Private Collection,
Ljubica Petrović, Belgrade

The Archers of Domagoj, 1917
plaster
Private Collection, London

The Archangel Gabriel, 1919
marble
Brooklyn Museum, New York

Mother and Child, 1922
marble
Fine Arts Gallery, San Diego

**Račić Family Memorial
Chapel,** 1922, stone
Cavtat

St. Francis of Assisi, 1924
bronze
Art Gallery, Dubrovnik

Female Nude
bronze, 42 cm
Meštrović Gallery, Split

Female nude
Charcoal drawing, 38 × 56 cm
Meštrović Gallery, Split

The Artist's Wife and Child
1924
bronze
Modern Gallery, Prague

My Mother at Prayer, 1926
marble
Art Institute, Chicago

Girl with a Lute, 1927
marble, 90 cm
Tate Gallery, London

Head of a Woman, 1927
bronze, 33 cm
Meštrović Gallery, Split

Cyclops, 1928
bronze, 23 cm
Meštrović Gallery, Split

Virgin and Child, 1928
diorite stone
Syracuse University

Angel with a Violin, 1929
wood
Artist's own Collection,
South Bend

Girl from Posavina, 1930
bronze, 195 cm
Meštrović Studio, Zagreb

Memorial of Thanks to France
1930
Kalemegdan Park, Belgrade

**Meštrović Family Memorial
Chapel,** 1931
Otavice

Meštrović Family Memorial
Chapel, 1931
stone
Otavice

Marica Meštrović, 1931
bronze, 42 cm
Meštrović Gallery, Split

St. Mark the Evangelist, 1932
stone
St. Mark's Church, Zagreb

Self-portrait, 1932
bronze, 55 cm
Meštrović Gallery, Split

Njegoš Mausoleum, 1932
first sketch
drawing

At Rest, 1933
bronze, 17 cm, sketch
Meštrović Gallery, Split

Vladimir Nazor, 1934
bronze 61 cm
Meštrović Gallery, Split

Unknown Warrior's Tomb,
1938, black granite
Avala, near Belgrade

Virgin and Child, detail 1937
bronze
Meštrović Gallery, Split

Unknown Warrior's Tomb,
1938, black granite
Avala, near Belgrade

Art Pavilion, 1939
today the Museum of the
Revolution
Trg žrtava fašizma, Zagreb

Art Pavilion, 1939
today the Museum of the
Revolution
Trg žrtava fašizma, Zagreb

St. Jerome, 1942
travertine
St. Jerome Institute, Rome

Pope Sisto V, 1942
travertine
St. Jerome Institute, Rome

Pope Pius XII, 1942
bronze
St. Jerome Institute, Rome

The Last Supper, 1945
oil on canvas, 95 × 117 cm
Meštrović Gallery, Split

Author of the Apocalypse
1946
travertine
St. Jerome Institute, Rome

The Family of Ivan Meštrović
1931
oil on wood, 95 × 117 cm
Meštrović Gallery, Split

Persephone, 1946
onyx
Marta Meštrović's Collection

Promethius, 1946
plaster, 67 cm, sketch
Artist's own Collection,
South Bend

Head of St. Christopher, 1947
plaster
Artist's own Collection,
South Bend

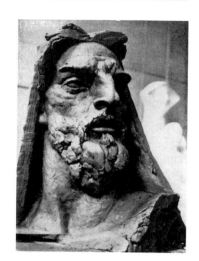

Isis and Horus, 1947
onyx
Artist's own Collection,
South Bend

Icarus, 1947
Artist's own Collection,
South Bend

The Prophet Jeremiah, 1952
stone
Artist's own Collection,
South Bend

Memorial to the Jewish Dead
1952, study
plaster

Head of a Boy
plaster
Tate Gallery, London

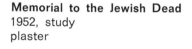

Study of Moses, 1953
plaster, 40 cm
Artist's own Collection,
South Bend

The Fall of Icarus, 1954
plaster, 31 cm
Artist's own Collection,
South Bend

The Return of the Prodigal Son
1954
plaster, 68 cm
Artist's own Collection,
South Bend

Head of Blind Homer, 1956
plaster
Artist's own Collection,
South Bend

Blind Homer, 1956
plaster, 40 cm
Artist's own Collection,
South Bend

Crucifixion, 1956
stone, 660 × 240 cm
The Church of the Trinity,
Rochester

Crucifixion, 1956
detail
The Church of the Trinity,
Rochester

Portrait of F. C. Morgan, 1957
bronze
Museum of Fine Arts,
Montreal

Jacob's Well, 1957
bronze
Notre Dame University,
South Bend

Mr. Thomas Beecham
bronze
London

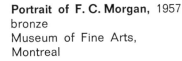

Prophet, 1956
plaster, 40 cm
Artist's own Collection,
South Bend

Memorial to Nadežda Petrović
bronze
Čačak

Andrija Kačić Miošić, 1957
bronze
Franciscan Monastery,
Zaostrog

Memorial to Father Lopez,
1958, bronze, 330 cm
Mission of nombre de dios
St. Augustine, Florida

Pieta, 1958
bronze
Miami, Florida

Petar Petrović Njegoš, 1958
granite, 364 cm
Cetinje

Mother and Child, 1946
onyx
Syracuse Museum of Fine Arts

Warriors, 1908
bronze, 67 × 200 cm
Meštrović Gallery, Split

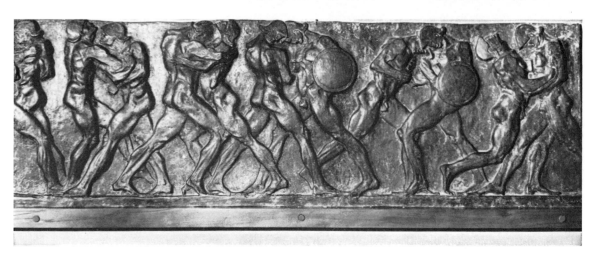

Meštrović Gallery (Split)

Meštrović Studio 1925 (Zagreb)

Kaštelet (Split)

Meštrović Studio (Zagreb)

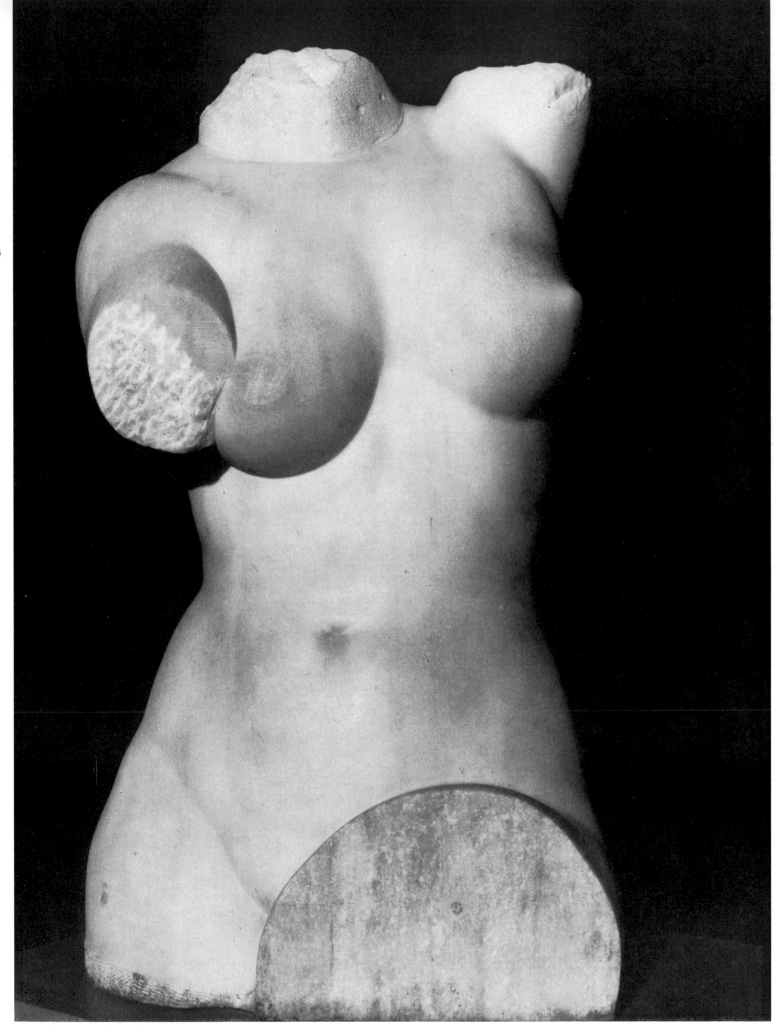

Selected Quotations from the Works of Meštrović

You would like to know how I came to change from national and historical subjects to biblical and religious ones. Here is a little explanation.

Anyone who has followed my work closely will see that my later work grows logically out of my earlier. This can be seen from what I said before. My nationalism was not an everyday affair, nor were the works I did at that time historical illustrations — they attempted to be an expression of the history of the soul of our nation, the soul which in its essence is general and human. I do not believe, and neither I think do you, that either individuals or nations are heroic if they fight simply for their own freedom or material gain, but only if they fight for general freedom and for general gain, and that cannot be on the material level. It is usual to think of military leaders as heroes, I hold that heroes are those who fight for the greatest ideals of humanity. You will no doubt agree with me if I say that I consider St. Paul a greater hero than Caesar.

Immediately after the Balkan War, and even more after the First World War I came to believe that the ideals of one nation are too small, the martyrdom or victory of one nation of too little significance in comparison with the martyrdom and victory of all. But the "victory of all" can only come if there are no more "friends" and "enemies", if we all feel ourselves to be brothers and human beings.

It was following the thread of these ideas and emotions that brought me to the Bible. A feeling for the general suffering of man then took a stronger place than for the suffering of a single nation. The need to overcome one particular evil, our evil, widened into need to overcome evil in general wherever it was and whosoever it was. These are old ideas and ideals. But one day they must be tried, and if they do not succeed today they may succeed tomorrow.

My newest things, those with the musical and melodic motifs, came out of a longing for general harmony. They are an expression of a desire for harmony between us and all things. It will be something if we manage even for a moment to achieve this harmony between us and all that is around us and above us. One day those will come who will achieve lasting harmony.

My art is expressed in hard wood and stone, but that which is in art is not in wood or stone, it is outside time and space. Art is a song and a prayer at the same time.

As in general humanity so in our national life I wish harmony to be achieved: harmony between people and the land in which they live and from which they live, between village and town, between the learned and the unlearned and above all harmony among our peoples. For love of this harmony I, in my own way, took part in the struggle for the freedom and unification of our nations, because I was convinced that in freedom we could best express the strength of our spirit and achieve a harmonious throbbing of strings. . .

"About My Art"
(Kolo, New York, 1924).

. . . I have such a high opinion of Michelangelo that I hardly dare to
write about him. If I nevertheless do it, I do it only to quieten my own
conscience for the frequent and the great experiences that I have had when
standing before his works. That is just why I do not dare to write about him,
but rather about the feelings that his works waken in me. . .

Our works in this world are the impression left by the wings of our souls,
which, though they are not eternal are the impress of an eternal being. The
wings of Michelangelo's soul were stronger, their flight was greater,
and so his works are greater and more lasting. When we think like this we
immediately bring to mind the Vatican Torso and compare it with
Michelangelo who so many times passed his hands over it. The Torso
in the passage of time, has lost its legs and arms and is still beautiful and
powerful, and so will his works be. From what is great, just a torso may
be left, and that for time illimitable, and from what is small nothing is left,
not even for now. From the great things we may break off the fingers and
then the arms and the legs. The torso is unbreakable. And in the small
things it is the torso that breaks first. That is where the difference lies
between one work and another! We must be in love with eternity, so that
our works are at least a shadow of it. What is eternal in us is shut up as
in a prison, we need to let it out into the light — into harmony with what is
deathless around us and above us. That is inspiration.

Love for the eternal is sacrifice, and sacrifice is seeking love for the eternal.
Evil is passing and good is passing. Blessedness is eternal and eternity is God.
The best way to fight against evil is to pray to God; and to struggle for the
beautiful means to sing his praises. It is written that in the beginning was the
word and the word was from God; but nowhere does it say whether the
word was written or carved. In any case art comes from a time when
the word was not separate from works, nor prayer from wisdom and song.
The true effort of artists should be a continuation of the cricket's song before
death, it should be song and prayer at the same time, and what it
contains should be outside dimensions and time — it should discover that
which others do not know and cannot see, and not copy that which others
see superficially and comprehend superficially. It should reveal truth that
is and not truth that seems to be.

■

. . . That part of art which we call "fine art", those whose effect is visual
and those which at least partly reach our mind through the eyes — architecture,
sculpture and painting — are composed of two elements: one of material
being, and one of spiritual being. These give them life. The material being
is spiritual and the spiritual invisible. They are thus the exact opposite
of each other. But things of this kind come to have meaning for us only
when the two elements fuse. For, however much what is material has
a factual existence, it does not exist as a building, a statue etc. until that
opposite element has christened it, fertilized it; just as that spiritual
element has a true existence in the mind, where it was born, but does not
exist for other eyes until it is combined with the material. When we say that
a work of art is harmonious, or perfect, or use some similar expression we
are in fact saying that it is formed of two elements which are in an equal
relationship the one with the other, so that they give us the idea of what
a particular art object in fact represents. What might those two elements
be other than the two we mentioned above: the spiritual and the
material. . .

. . . Perhaps (in this extrasensual aspect) all kinds of ideas unknown and
ununderstood by us affect the quality of the work: the longings and
feelings of our forebears in ancient generations, their virtues and vices.
In what way this may happen and how great such an influence may be is
something we do not know.

... For this reason true art is, in essence, similar to nature. Its source is a mystery as is the source of our life, but it is the same source. This means that the spiritual is part of the affirmation of life, it is the necessary affirmation, the voice and the song of emotional life, and at the same time of physical, and takes on form as life does, so that it becomes apparent to our physical senses. This spiritual life is the witness that mankind as a whole is eternal however transient the individual may be.

... Each art, when it is great, has elements of the others: music has the constructive elements of architecture and sculpture, and the colours of painting; the plastic arts have rhythm and melody. True poetry has elements from them all, and in fact is a combination of all of them together. We hardly need to point out that pictures have architectural construction and sculptural plasticity; and the same is true in the opposite sense of architecture and sculpture and, above the real forms, the illusion of painting. Nevertheless each branch needs to accent its own particular kind, for when this is not so then art is colourless, blurred, characterless and dishonest. This does not happen to art that is created spontaneously, instinctively and intuitively, but most often with works created intellectually, without true inspiration, as speculation not inspiration; the author of such works has made a mistake in his choice of language — and for this reason, in their expressive aims, their true kind is not sufficiently stressed.

Art has always been part of what is finest in man and gone in step with his greatest aspirations in the idealistic and moral sense...

... Michelangelo is one of the typical fathers of modern man, who struggled with his whole being, bones, flesh and nerves, with his questing and beliefs, to rise to the divine and thus convince himself that man is, after all, part of eternity.

"Michelangelo",
New Europe, 1926.

Acquaintances sometimes ask me what it is that makes me stay here: what has been accepted of all that I proposed? Have I anything in common with the world here, and do I find understanding? What in fact is it that I am looking for here among you?

I tell them that I want to show that here one can live too, I want to show that this small corner of the world is just as near to, or just as far from, the forces that move the world as any other, in fact for me it is nearer than any other. I believe that each one of us needs to work in their own country among their own people, giving from themselves and of themselves...

I believe that the sun will come out and warm the earth. I believe that women will bear children and the fields crops. I believe that love and blistered hands will always build and not destroy. It is only the mindless and the parasites that destroy. I believe that evil men will not prevent the good. I believe that chemistry will not destroy and neither will it lead to the salvation of mankind. I believe that prosperity is not the prime mover of the world and that stock exchanges, banks and customs barriers will not bring harmony, nor wealth nor justice... I believe that we shall not be the last among the last, but slowly come to be equal with the best. And finally I believe that this white town of ours will become all that it is not yet, because that is what the people want, and they will bring to it their heart and brain just as now they bring to it everything from which it lives.

Preface to catalogue
of exhibition in Zagreb, 1932.

My contemporaries are not dangerous, I am neither afraid of them nor ashamed, but of "those who were" and "those who will be", — the examination that concerns me is the one that comes when all labels have disappeared. For me this is something that cannot be explained by my particular case, nor time nor circumstances, although they are all part of the reason.

Almost all that you see here in reproduction is nothing more than notes, sketches and studies, preparations for all that which I wanted to say more completely and fully. For that reason I feel that my finest sculptures will remain in the hills in the cliffs, undiscovered — at least by me — and that on them eagles will rest, and will consider and measure the height from which the sun's rays strike, which give life and call to them. I from the upper layers only, that are burned by the sun and bitten by the storms and by time, have hewn out models for those real figures that are contained in huge blocks. There is no excuse for me, I had the lever in my hands like others long before me whose work came out of greater depths.

■

Besides that my true ambition in my work was not to be the first in my own country, for I very early realized that even a little tree is very easy to see where there is no forest. That was the reason why I was so often unreasonable at home and even seemed strange. As soon as I could stand on my own feet I truly desired to go beyond my contemporaries for I very clearly saw how small they and I were in comparison with those whole pleiads from the past. What I had come to realize, and what I wanted to achieve very quickly, brought me to a position in which, even abroad, I was not contemporary. Abroad one group think that we have discovered a new content for art, another group that the really creative times have long gone by. I did not agree with either: I never did believe that God stopped creating on the seventh day, nor have I ever thought that anything, physical or spiritual — can be free of the inherited. I have never hated the times in which I live, nor unestimated them, but I have tried not to overestimate them either and not to separate them from times gone by, but — as far as I can — link them with past times and see them as a preparation for future times, always fostering enthusiasm for times to come, which needs must be better and more beautiful than these times. In all the works of our forebears I read that they had the same feeling. A spiritual and emotional link always leads us all to the same sources which are always the same, however much their noise and colour may vary — their flow and pressure is the same. When we try to find total harmony in what we call justice, truth, beauty, wisdom, divided up in this way they glimmer like fireflies and are gone. The real guide is faith, for faith demands our life, and real life demands faith, since in faith it may live. That is why the true and only goals of art, and of all other spiritual human strivings, are eternal, like life, and inseparable from life. And the value of art lies in how, and how much it is linked to those goals.

■

As in other things so too in art our century is not the worst, only it suffers more than other centuries from a longing for what it is not, and from imagining that it is what it is not. For example, in no previous century has so much been written about the individual and the original, and in almost no century has there been less that in fact is individual and original...

I have never thought that art should serve any ideology or system which is in oposition to the national spirit or belief; and still less that true art can be produced either against or without the personal belief of the person creating it. In the same way it cannot be an illustration either of historical fact or of legend if it does not also contain some personal life and feeling and witness. I agree with those who say that art must be free from the interference of an autocracy and a false democracy, and of doctrinaire religion; but I can absolutely believe that those anonymous men who worked on the French cathedrals worked of their free will and with full belief, like all true artists before and after them who believed in the forms and figures they were creating. It was belief of this kind that led me in my sculpture of national subjects and subjects from history. I was never sorry for having done either, nor did I find such obstacles as some people think, for every small tragedy is similar to some big one, and we humans from time immemorial have felt the human to be like the divine.

Preface to the monograph,
Meštrović, 1933.

What people have written about Meštrović

Auguste Rodin.

Meštrović is the greatest phenomenon among sculptors.

■

Maksim Gorki,
in a letter to S. M. Prohorov, 1911.

I have personally found the Rome exhibition very interesting and have gained a lot from it . . . I am also impressed by the very good Serbian sculptor Meštrović.

■

Emile Verhaeren,
Belgian writer.

One of the dominating personalities of art history.

■

James Bone,
British art critic, 1919.

Ivan Meštrović, having the fortune to spend his early days in a land throbbing with unwearied poetry and touching on every side the primitive realities of suffering and life and death, began with that great advantage and required no search for a subject. It was in the air about him and in the dreams of his countrymen — the martyrdom of the Serbs. For almost the first time in modern art a rare and powerful talent was working in the service of profound national emotion.

■

Josef Strzygowski,
Austrian art historian,
professor of Vienna University,
1924.

The South Slavs have the incredible fortune that at what perhaps is the most important moment of their history they have a great artist steeped in the blood, in the earth in the fate of his country.

. . . The works of Meštrović contain the strength of a new birth, they awake respect wherever they are exhibited, and we repeat, for the last time, — that superficial judgments that content themselves with stating like or dislike are beside the point. One thing that is certain is that for the first time in the works of Meštrović Yugoslav art has attained world fame.

■

Kineton Parkes,
English art historian and critic,
1925.

One of the most powerful constructive artists on the world scene is Ivan Meštrović, the Yugoslav sculptor-architect, who began life as a shepherd boy, and who now strongly affects contemporary life with his discovery of new truths and new beauty. He speaks in a way that can be understood by all for whom art is a reality and not simply a skill.

Rodin came at the end of a period that was in decline. Meštrović has come at the beginning of one that is original and fertile: and he is one of its most important and most outstanding representatives.

. . . When he entered the arena of European art he was a masterly and an original artist.

Work like his has never been seen before. It has many qualities rare in modern art, and the most important of these is: passion. He was impelled by a powerful need to express himself and an unbridled impulse to create what his spirit dictated. He needed only to overcome physical obstacles, there were no spiritual ones.

Meštrović's exhibition at the Victoria and Albert Museum has been a discovery for artists too, and not only for the British public.

■

Milan Marjanović,
Croatian writer and journalist,
1925.

With his art, his exhibitions and his personal contacts, from the 1911 Rome Exhibition down to the end of the war, Meštrović has done more for the reputation of his country than scores of diplomats and political propaganda experts. Nor has he done less than in their heroism his fellow countrymen on the battle fields.

■

. . . His language, his wood pictures, and his gesture remind you of the guslar, the Yugoslav minstrel, reciting some ancient ballads.

Mihajlo Pupin,
Serbian physicist,
professor of Columbia University,
New York, 1925.

He is the ideal type of the best which a Yugoslav village can produce. A lovely type, representing as it does an embodiment of all the Christian virtues of which the guslar sings. Sincerity, humility, charity, love are the predominant notes in his art.

Ante Tresić Pavičić,
Croatian writer, 1925.

Meštrović is not only a great artist, but a very profound thinker. He is a Proteus in everlasting evolution, always the same yet always different, like the time and the ambient atmosphere in which he works. He tries to express all the sentiments and aspirations, not only of his nation but of humanity.
He belongs not only to our nation, but to all nations and to all times.

Branko Lazarević,
Serbian writer, 1927.

The Cavtat Memorial Chapel is pain in Brač limestone. The whole mausoleum is an expression of death and sorrow in stone. Except for the basic shape, which is too stark, rational and balanced to be completely religious and, painful, everything else — particularly the figures and the ornaments, from the angels and the entrance pillars, the reliefs on the doors and the bell to the Virgin and St. Roch — everything else is weighted down by a secret sorrow and suffering, under a religion which is so much the religion of death, of general death and general decay, that it is no longer Christian, except in form. It is not so much farewell and peace be to man as a general pagan, pantheistic farewell to everything and peace be to all and everything. This chapel is not religious in the narrow sense; it provides a broad, profound and general religious experience the width and depth of which seem part of a general philosophy of death.

Miroslav Krleža,
Croatian writer, 1928.

... In the earlier phases of his development, in his moments of pure, unsullied inspiration Meštrović's works relied on unencumbered, clean line, the traditional realization of material form. Many of his works demonstrate that sculpture, the embodiment of the human form, has not and cannot have any other goal than to arrest the passing, to petrify movement and to objectify the body, to give material form to the transient somatic object. He mastered all the problems of sculpture with the ease and instinct of a gifted man, and many of his statues are sculpturally solved with the simple formulas of the multiplication table where twice two are four.

But, parallel with this clarity, from the very beginning Meštrović has been in love with the instinctive, the obscure. In all the opacity of his biblical vocabulary (in which he has written his most recent composition about Michelangelo), he likes to envelop his statues as if they were in winding sheets. This was and has remained the typical Vienna Secession religiosity in him.

Ljubo Babić,
Croatian painter
and art historian, 1943.

The essential characteristic and the deep meaning of his nature was that it came from the most profound level of his being like some great original power. It was as if enormous strength had for centuries been supressed and had to force its way up from beneath the surface, beneath stone, beneath the impoverished and naked Karst to seek its own inevitable forms. It sought those forms with a power seldom equalled in the history of art.

Sought harmony, twisting across the uneven terrain of our country like some torrent carrying with it a whole lot of irrelevant things, decoratism and all the burden of centuries, the ballast of foreign expressions and moulds. A forest of granite, marble, bronze wood and plaster has been the record of that tragic and difficult journey. The greatness and the tragedy of Ivan Meštrović do not lie in the fact that he is an artist of a small nation, his greatness and tragedy are in his work as a whole. His entire sublimated life with all its positive and negative elements was a concentrated urge to break through to his own form of expression, special and completely different from any other either among his contemporaries or his forerunners. The existence of that strength and the method of its break through sets an artistic problem before us. In so far as Meštrović solved it, then our art has taken its place on the pages of world history, still more, as a native plant it has gained its meaning and its justification.

Margaret Crossen,
American art critic, 1947.

In times like ours, when the accent is largely on power, money, science and material progress, it seems to be very rare for an artist to appear who has all the marks of a genius. Genius is an essential part of the human spirit. It is very different from talent. Talent is measurable. To a certain extent it can be attained by hard work and ambition. Genius, on the contrary, comes forth completely developed. It is full and complete at birth. Those who possess it have no choice. They work because they have to work. They are artists because they can be nothing else. It is among these that Meštrović belonged.

It is singularly significant that he is almost unanimously revered by American sculptors of all schools as one of "the greatest living sculptors"!

... Though he studied, worked and exhibited in Austria, Italy, France, England the United States, he cannot be classified as belonging to one or another, and yet he has been a part of all these nationalities, their traditions and their faiths. He was Croatian, and what he tried to express was rooted in the heart and soil of his homeland. Its successful achievement, however, was not in any one language, but rather in that of all humanity.

Alonzo Lansford,
American art critic, 1947.

It is difficult to believe that so many great projects have been conceived and carried to their ultimate completion by one man.

Malvina Hoffman,
American sculpturess, 1947.

There is an unmistakable influence of pre-classical and classical sculpture in the work of this modern master. There is no attempt in his work to cast aside the past in favour of some currently fashionable notion. But if the past is present in this sculpture, there is an element of the future as well; the major works of Meštrović have a quality of timelessness which does not depend on either past style or current fashion for their artistic strength.

Norman L. Rice,
Head of the Art School,
University of Syracuse, 1948.

This sculptor brings to his works the knowledge of a lifetime and to his subject a personal understanding of vicissitudes and pathos.

Dorothy Adlow,
American art critic, 1951.

After we have paid all due tribute to the founders of modern art there are still reasons for believing that the figurative art that Meštrović is still putting before the world will continue to be fresh and forceful when non-figurative works will be mainly remembered from the histories of art... His great richness lies in the fact that his works are charged with emotional content, far from the cold, unexpressive, remote works of the too abstract sculptors...

Ivan Meštrović has become a legend. And in his creative work, which has hardly any parallel in the contemporary world, his works sculpture for themselves.

George A. Cevasco,
American art critic, 1959.

Laurence Schmeckebier,
Director of Art School,
Syracuse University,
and author of **Ivan Meštrović**,
1959.

That Meštrović is a major figure in the sculpture of the twentieth century there can be no question. Indeed the judgement of time will place him among the great sculptors of history.

Žarko Vidović, Author of
**Meštrović
and the Contemporary
conflict between Sculpture
and Arhitecture**, 1961.

In one sense we can consider Meštrović to be one of the key figures in contemporary sculpture. If we except Rodin from the Secessionist movement, since he was linked to it only formally through exhibitions and the large number of his followers among German expressionists, then Meštrović was the greatest figure of that movement.

This master sculptor of our times is of the same company as the great masters of the past. To those who worked in the tradition of western humanism, beginning with the great Greeks, continuing on through the Renaissance and the powerful genius of Michelangelo and in more recent time Rodin and Bourdelle, we may now add the name of Ivan Meštrović... We are glad that this great artist chose to pass the last days of his life in this country and with us.

Donald de Lue,
editor New York
National Sculpture Review, 1962.

It is difficult to judge the importance of the works of a Meštrović in the art of the South Slav nations. He was their greatest artist, he drew the attention of the whole world to the fate of the South Slav peoples, and he consciously used his creative gifts in the service of this high ideal... His finest sculptures, real and convincing, were conceived in memory of the great heroes of the past and their manly struggle for freedom. Meštrović was inspired by the desire for the unification of the South Slavs into a single, independent national state. His art has found expression in the works of contemporary Yugoslav sculptors not so much because of his example of skilful workmanship, as for his patriotic services to his people, his homeland.

Igor K. Tupicin,
Soviet art historian,
author of a monograph
on Meštrović, 1967.

And the past? Meštrović has died but the presence of his spirit in sculpture, shines upon this land even today - from St. Marko in Zagreb to Meje on the Adriatic Coast, to Avala, to Kalemegdan.

Joja Ricov,
Croatian writer and arts critic,
1963.

Ivan Meštrović

Select bibliography

⊥ = Page | No. = Nummer | □ = Volume

Ivan Meštrović:

1
O umjetnosti. Pokret I/1904, No. 28.

Ivan Meštrović:

2
Ivan Meštrović. Monographie. Kunst, Wien, II/1904, □ 8.

Ivan Meštrović

3
Misli jednog kipara. Lovor, Zadar, 1905, ⊥ 91.

Josip Kosor:

4
Ivan Meštrović. Impresije. Pokret III/1906, No. 87.

5
Das Werk des Bildhauers Ivan Meštrović. Erdgeist, Wien, III/1908, □ 1—2. (Prijevod: Sloboda, Split, 2, 16. V 1908).

6
Izložba Medulića. Katalog, Zagreb 1910.

Antun Gustav Matoš:

7
Meštrović. Horvatska sloboda III/1910, No. 101—103.

Arthur Rössler:

8
Ivan Meštrović. Deutsche Kunst und Dekoration. Darmstadt, XIII/1910, □ 9.

Ivo Vojnović:

9
Akordi. Savremenik, Zagreb, V/1910, No. 5, ⊥ 301, br. 8, ⊥ 556.

A. M(ilčinović):

10
Ivan Meštrović. Živopisna crtica. Savremenik, Zagreb, V/1910, No. 5, ⊥ 306.

(Arthur Rössler) ss:

11
Ivan Meštrović. Bildende Künstler, Wien, 1911, □ 1, ⊥ 14.

Vittorio Pica:

12
L'Arte mondiale a Roma nel 1911. Bergamo 1913.

Jerolim Miše:

13
Ivan Meštrović. Sloboda, Split, 7, 12. V, 19. VI 1914.

James Bone:

14
Ivan Meštrović. Exhibition of the works of Ivan Meštrović. London 1915.

Milan Marjanović:

15
Genij jugoslovenstva Ivan Meštrović i njegov hram. New York 1915.

A. Yusuf Ali:

16
Meštrović and Serbian Sculpture. London 1916.

Momčilo Selesković:

17
Ivan Meštrović. Misao, Oxford, I/1919, No. 4, ⊥ 97.

J. Lavery, M. Ćurčin,
I. Vojnović, J. Bone,
B. Popović, E. Collings,
R. W. Seton Watson:

18
Ivan Meštrović. A Monograph. London 1919.

Ivan Strajnić:

19
Ivan Meštrović. Beograd 1919.

Josip Kosor:

20
Ivan Meštrović. Nova Evropa, Zagreb, I/1920, No. 13, ⊥ 439.

(Ivan Meštrović):

21
Zamisao Kosovskog hrama. Nova Evropa, Zagreb, I/1922, No. 13, ⊥ 447.

Ivan Meštrović

Select bibliography

⊥ = Page | No. = Nummer | □ = Volume

22
J. Lavery: **Meštrović u Engleskoj.** Nova Evropa, Zagreb, I/1920, No. 13, ⊥ 418.

23
Josef Strzygowski: **Eine Grabkirche von Ivan Meštrović.** Deutsche Kunst und Dekoration, Darmstadt, 1923, □ 9.

24
Gustav Krklec: **Meštrović i Plečnik. Dva velika uspeha naših umetnika u inostranstvu.** Srpski književni glasnik, Beograd, IX/1923, No. 7, ⊥ 543.

25
Christian Brinton: **The Meštrović Exhibition.** New York 1924.

26
Meštrović pred licem sveta. (Svezak posvećen Meštroviću). Nova Evropa, Zagreb, X/1924, No. 1

27
Josip Strzygowski: **Meštrovićevo mesto u razvoju svetske umetnosti.** Nova Evropa X/1924, No. 1, ⊥ 2.

28
James Bone: **Meštrovićeva umetnost.** Nova Evropa, Zagreb, X/1924, No. 1, ⊥ 10.

29
S. Kordić: **Umetnost i neumetnost.** Povodom umetnosti Ivana Meštrovića. Beograd 1924.

M. Pupin, F. Bruguiere,
A. Tresić-Pavičić,
I. Meštrović,
M. Marjanović,
P. Karović:
30
Ivan Meštrović Number. The Yugoslav Review, New York, III/1925, No. 2.

31
Milan Marjanović: **Preci i mladost Ivana Meštrovića.** New York 1925.

32
Kineton Parkes: **Ivan Meštrović skulptor-arhitekt.** Srpski književni glasnik, Beograd, XV/1925, No. 5, ⊥ 367.

33
(Ivan Meštrović): **Meštrović o svojoj umjetnosti.** Novo doba, Split, 13. II 1925.

34
Ivan Meštrović: **Mikelanđelo.** Uvod u studiju. Nova Evropa, Zagreb, 1926, No. 9—10, ⊥ 243.

35
Kosta Strajnić: **Svetosavski hram.** Javni apel ... Beograd 1926.

36
Miroslav Krleža: **O Ivanu Meštroviću.** Književnik, Zagreb, I/1928, No. 3, ⊥ 73.

37
Oskar Schürer: **Werke von Ivan Meštrović.** Die Kunst, München, 1927/28, No. 57, ⊥ 182.

38
Frane Bulić: **O položaju Grgura Ninskoga u Splitu.** Jadranska pošta, Split, 2. V 1929.

39
Ljubo Karaman: **O Grguru Ninskome i Meštrovićevu spomeniku u Splitu.** Split 1929.

40
Rudolf Sieber: **Grgur Ninski. Ein Denkmal von I. Meštrović in Split.** Jugoslavenski turizam, Split, 1929, ⊥ 392.

41
Raymond Warnier: **Mechtrovitch et ses oeuvres recentes.** Gazette des Beaux-Arts, Paris, octobre 1930.

Select bibliography

⊥ = Page | No. = Nummer | □ = Volume

Branko Lazarević:
42
Tri najviše jugoslavenske vrednosti. Beograd 1930.

H. Tietze:
43
Meštrović's Denkmal des Bischofs Gregor von Nin. Deutsche Kunst und Dekoration, Darmstadt, 1931, No. 69.

44
Ivan Meštrović. IV. kolektivna izložba. Katalog. Zagreb 1932.

Heinrich Ritter:
45
Ivan Meštrović. Deutsche Kunst und Dekoration, Darmstadt, XXXV/1932, □ 10.

Josef Strzygowski:
46
Eine Grabkirche von Ivan Meštrović. Deutsche Kunst und Dekoration, Darmstadt, XXXV/1932, □ 10.

47
Exposition Ivan Meštrović. Paris 1933, Katalog.

Fr. Táborsky:
48
Ivan Meštrović. Praha 1933. Monografija.

Ivan Meštrović, Milan Ćurčin:
49
Meštrović. Zagreb 1933. Monografija.

Raimond Warnier:
50
Le statuaire Ivan Meštrović et son oeuvre. Revue de l'Art Ancien et Moderne, 1933, No. 63.

Louis Adamic:
51
The native's return. New York 1934.

A. St. Magr:
52
Meštrović, der südslawische Bildhauer. Leipzig 1935.

A. St. Magr:
53
Mestrovic. Literatur. Slawische Rundschau, Brünn, 1935, □ VII.

Ivan Meštrović:
54
Umetnikova ispovijest. Jadranski dnevnik, Split, 20. IV 1935.

Vojeslav Molè:
55
Ivan Meštrović. Monografija. Krakow 1936.

Ivan Meštrović:
56
Gospa od anđela. Monografija. Zagreb 1937.

Ivan Meštrović:
57
Quelques souvenirs sur Rodin. Annales de l'Institut français de Zagreb, Zagreb, I/1937, No. 1, ⊥ 3.

Robert M. Murko:
58
Spomenik neznanom junaku na Avali. Nova Evropa, Zagreb, XXXI/1938, No. 12, ⊥ 386.

Vičo Ivanov:
59
Ivan Meštrović i njegovoto izkustvo. Plovdiv 1938.

Cvito Fisković:
60
Meštrovićeva djela u Splitu. Glasnik Primorske banovine, Split, I/1938, No. 2, ⊥ 14.

Ivan Zemljak:
61
Dom likovnih umjetnosti u Zagrebu. Građevinski vjesnik, Zagreb, VIII/1939, No. 2, ⊥ 17.

Ivan Meštrović

Select bibliography

⊥ = Page | No. = Nummer | □ = Volume

62
Ivan Meštrović: **Nekoliko uspomena na Rodina.** Hrvatski glasnik, Split, 1939, No. 84.

63
(Sokrates Stavropulos): **Heroische Bildhauerkunst.** Fünf Werke von Ivan Meštrović. Budapest 1939.

64
Milan Crnjanski: **Meštrović, der markanteste Bildhauer Jugoslawiens.** Freude und Arbeit, Berlin, 1939.

65
Josip Strzygowski: **La place d'Ivan Meštrović dans l'art universel.** L'echo de Belgrade, Beograd, 1. XII 1940.

66
Ljubo Babić: **Umjetnost kod Hrvata.** Zagreb 1943.

67
Ivan Meštrović: **Religiozna umjetnost.** Zagreb 1944. Monografija.

68
Ivan Meštrović: **Dennoch will ich hoffen.** Zürich 1945.

69
Malvina Hoffman: **»Where there is no Vision the People Perish«.** Liturgical Arts, New York, XV/1947, No. 4, ⊥ 89.

70
Duško Kečkemet: **Hrvatska moderna plastika.** Urbanizam i arhitektura, Zagreb 1950, No. 3—4, ⊥ 65.

71
Ivan Meštrović: **Imaginarni razgovori s Mikelanđelom.** Odlomci. Hrvatska revija, Buenos Aires, I/1951, □ 3, 205, III/1953, □ 1, ⊥ 43, X/1960, □ 10, ⊥ 503.

Norman L. Rice,
Harry H. Hilberry,
72
Estelle S. Hilberry: **The Sculpture of Ivan Meštrović.** Syracuse, 1948. Monografija.

73
Rudolf Sieber: **Ivan Meštrović.** Kunst ins Volk, Wien, V/1953—1954, □ 1/2, ⊥ 37.

74
Ivan Ćurčin: **Meštrović u Americi.** Arhitektura, Zagreb, 1953, No. 4.

75
The Life of Christ. Ten Panels in Wood by Ivan Meštrović. Syracuse (1953). Mape.

76
Duško Kečkemet: **Školovanje i prva djela Ivana Meštrovića u Splitu.** Slobodna Dalmacija, Split, 21. X 1953.

77
Ivan Meštrović: **Gespräche mit Michelangelo.** Kunst ins Volk, Wien, VI—IX/1955—1958, □ 1/4, 5/6—7/8, 9/10—12.

78
Duško Kečkemet: **Bibliografija o Splitu.** Split 1956. Ivan Meštrović, ⊥ 119.

79
Katalog Galerije Ivana Meštrovića u Splitu. Split 1957.

80
Laurence Schmeckebier: **Ivan Meštrović, Sculptor and Patriot.** Syracuse 1959. Monografija.

Duško Kečkemet,
81
Kruno Prijatelj: **Počeci Ivana Meštrovića.** Split 1959.

82
Katarina Ambrozić: **Paviljon Srbije na međunarodnoj izložbi u Rimu 1911. godine.** Zbornik radova Narodnog muzeja. Beograd 1962, No. 3.

Ivan Meštrović

Text: Duško Kečkemet
Photography: Milan Babić, Tošo Dabac, Marjan Pfeifer, Branko Turin
Art editor: Jože Brumen
Selection and arrangement: Dragutin Zdunić, Jože Brumen
Editor: Dragutin Zdunić
Expert adviser: Josip Smrkinić
English Translation: Sonia Wild Bićanić
Publishers: »Spektar«, Zagreb — ČGP »Delo«, Ljubljana
Printed by: ČGP »Delo«, Ljubljana, Yugoslavia, 1970
Edition in 30,000 copies, published in Serbo-Croatian, Slovenian, English, German, French, Italian and Russian

Select bibliography

⊥ = Page | No. = Nummer | □ = Volume

George A. Cevasco:
83
The Legend of Ivan Mestrovic. American Artist, New York 1959, □ 23, No. 4, ⊥ 34, 95.

Ivan Meštrović:
84
Uspomene na političke ljude i događaje. Buenos Aires 1961.

Žarko Vidović:
85
Meštrović i savremeni sukob skulptora s arhitektom. Sarajevo 1961.

Željko Grum:
86
Ivan Meštrović. Zagreb 1961. Monografija. (Fotografije Tošo Dabac).

F. Vyncke:
87
L'esprit slave et universel d'Ivan Meštrović. La lampe verte, Bruxelles, I/1962.

Duško Kečkemet:
88
Umjetnost Ivana Meštrovića. Mogućnosti, Split, IX/1962, No. 3, ⊥ 254.

Duško Kečkemet:
89
Umjetnost Ivana Meštrovića. Split 1962.

Vesna Novak-Oštrić:
90
Društvo hrvatskih umjetnika »Medulić« 1908—1916. Zagreb 1962. Katalog izložbe.

I. Meštrović, J. Kljaković, M. Meštrović, B. Radica, Z. Tomičić, S. Vujica, D. Mandić, R. Kupareo, A. Nizeteo, K. Mirth, N. Kesterčanek:
91
Ivan Meštrović. (1883—1962). Hrvatska revija, Buenos Aires, XII/1962, □ 4, ⊥ 297.

92
Ivan Meštrović. Zagreb 1963. Katalog Ateljea Meštrović. Tekst Vesna Barbić.

Duško Kečkemet:
93
Ivan Meštrović. Beograd 1964. Monografija. (Fotografije Tošo Dabac).

94
Meštrović, Ivan. Enciklopedija likovnih umjetnosti, Zagreb 1964, □ 3, ⊥ 444.

Zlatko Tomičić:
95
Put k Meštroviću. Buenos Aires 1965.

Igor K. Tupicin:
96
Ivan Meštrović. Moskva 1967. Monografija.

97
Galerija Meštrović. Katalog. Split 1967. Tekst Josip Smrkinić, Duško Kečkemet.

Ivan Meštrović:
98
Uspomene na političke ljude i događaje. Zagreb, 1969.

Joja Ricov:
99
Lettera dalla Jugoslavia, D'Ars Agency, N° 5, Milano 1963.

1
Selfportrait, detail, 1932
Bronze, 55 cm
Meštrović Gallery, Split

2
My Mother, 1909
Bronze, 37 cm
Meštrović Gallery, Split

3
Cyclops, 1933
Bronze, 249 cm
Meštrović Gallery, Split

4
Bishop Gregory of Nin, detail

5
Bishop Gregory of Nin, 1927
Bronze, 750 cm
Opposite north gate of Diocletian's Palace,
Split

6
Marko Marulić, detail, 1924
Bronze, 58 cm
Split Municipal Museum
Meštrović Studio, Zagreb (plaster)

7
Marko Marulić, 1924
Bronze, 265 cm
Trg preporoda, Split

8
The Well of Life, 1905
Bronze, 108 cm
Marshal Tito Square, Zagreb

9
The Well of Life, detail

10
Slave, 1908
Bronze, 73 cm
National Museum, Belgrade

11
Petar Petrović Njegoš, 1958
Detail of the granite figure
Cetinje

12
Unknown Warrior's Tomb, detail

13
Caryatids on the Unknown Warrior's Tomb, 1938
Granite
Avala, near Belgrade

14
Selfportrait, detail, 1941
Bronze, 48 cm
Meštrović Gallery, Split

15
Josip Juraj Strossmayer, 1926
Bronze, 350 cm
Strossmayerov trg, Zagreb

16
St. John the Evangelist, 1929
Bronze, 187 cm
Meštrović Studio, Zagreb

17
Ruđer Bošković
Plaster
Glyptotheca, Zagreb
Ruđer Bošković Institute, Zagreb, Bronze

18
Goethe, 1932
Bronze, 62 cm
Meštrović Studio, Zagreb

19
Luka Botić
One variant of the Statue, 1905
Plaster, 117 cm
Art Gallery, Split

20
Nikola Tesla
bronze
Ruđer Bošković Institute, Zagreb

21
Tomislav Krizman, 1905
Plaster, 91 cm
Glyptotheca, Zagreb

22—23
Miloš Obilić, 1908
Bronze, 260 cm
National Museum, Belgrade

24
Miloš Obilić, detail

25
Mate Meštrović, 1941
Bronze, 46 cm
Meštrović Gallery, Split

26
Meštrović's Chapel, door frame with family portraits, 1934
Otavice

27
Indian with Spear, 1927
Bronze, 600 cm
Grant Park, Chicago

28
Lamentation, 1931
Bronze, 114 × 190 cm
Meštrović Gallery, Split

29
Man and Freedom, 1953
Bronze, 720 cm
Mayo Clinic, Rochester

30
Indian with Bow, 1927
Bronze, 600 cm
Grant Park, Chicago

31
Indian with Spear, 1927
Bronze, 600 cm
Grant Park, Chicago

32
The Sculptor at Work — Rodin
Rome, 1914
Meštrović Gallery, Zagreb

33
Krajević Marko, head, 1910
Bronze
National Museum, Belgrade

34
Kraljević Marko, sketch, 1911
Bronze, 40 cm
Meštrović Gallery, Split

35
Soldier's Head, 1908
Bronze, 82 cm
Meštrović Gallery, Split

36
John the Baptist, 1914
Bronze, 59.5 cm
Meštrović Gallery, Split
Gallery of Modern Art, Zagreb

37
Portrait of Dinko Šimunović
Plaster
Owned by Frano Šimunović

38
Luke the Evangelist, detail

39
Luke the Evangelist, 1914
Bronze, 59 cm
Meštrović Gallery, Split

40
Vladimir Becić, 1932
Bronze, 66 cm
Meštrović Gallery, Split
Gallery of Modern Art, Zagreb
Mirogoj Cemetery, Zagreb

41
Anguish, 1946
Bronze, 96 cm
Meštrović Gallery, Split
Artist' own Collection, South Bend

42
Male Torse, 1932
Bronze, 98 cm
Meštrović Gallery, Split

43
Job, 1946
Bronze, 122 cm
Meštrović Gallery, Split
Syracuse University

44
Girl with a Lute, 1918
Bronze, 77 cm
Meštrović Gallery, Split

45
Female Nude
Bronze, 37 cm
Meštrović Gallery, Split

46
Happy Youth, 1946
Bronze, 196 cm
Artist's own Collection, South Bend
Meštrović Gallery, Split

47
Atlantis, 1946
Bronze, 186 cm
Artist's own Collection, South Bend
Meštrović Gallery, Split

48
Widow and Child, 1912
Bronze, 175 cm
National Museum, Belgrade

49
Angel with a Flute, 1918
Bronze, 137 cm
Gallery of Modern Art, Zagreb

50
Virgin and Child, 1937
Bronze, 152 cm
Meštrović Gallery, Split

51
Ruža Meštrović, 1915
Bronze, 85 cm
Meštrović Gallery, Split
Gallery of Modern Art, Zagreb

52
Virgin and Child, 1917
Bronze, 105 cm
Meštrović Gallery, Split

53
Lamentation, 1914
Bronze, 46 cm
Meštrović Gallery, Split

54
Distant Chords, 1918
Bronze, 227 cm
Meštrović Gallery, Split

55
Vestal Virgin, 1917
Bronze, 128 cm
Meštrović Gallery, Split

56
Woman Praying, 1917
Bronze, 51 cm
Meštrović Gallery, Split

57
Boy with a Bird, 1934
Bronze, 55 cm
Meštrović Gallery, Split

58
Caryatid's Head, 1934
Red granite, 80 cm
Meštrović Studio, Zagreb

59
Girl with a Violin, 1922
Marble, 51 cm
Meštrović Gallery, Split

60
In Despair, 1927
Marble, 117 cm
Meštrović Gallery, Split

61
Woman with a Harp, 1924
Marble, 193×70 cm
Meštrović Gallery, Split

Woman with a Lute, 1924
Marble, 183×68 cm
Meštrović Gallery, Split

62
My Mother, 1908
Marble, 97 cm
National Museum, Belgrade

63
The History of the Croats, 1932
Stone, 168 cm
Meštrović Studio, Zagreb
Belgrade

64
Woman Beside the Sea, 1926
Marble
Meštrović Studio, Zagreb
Meštrović Gallery, Split (bronze)

65
A Mother Dedicates her Child, 1927
Marble, 106 cm
Meštrović Gallery, Split

66
Widow, 1908
Marble, 160 cm
National Museum, Belgrade

67
Widow, 1908
Marble
National Museum, Belgrade

68
Memories, 1908
Marble, 150 cm
National Museum, Belgrade

69
Memories, detail

70
Dreaming, 1927
Stone, 88×188 cm
Meštrović Gallery, Split

71
Psyche, 1927
Marble, 208 cm
Meštrović Gallery, Split

72
Psyche, detail

73
Woman's Torso, 1927
Marble, 110 cm
Meštrović Studio, Zagreb

74
Ruža Meštrović
Marble

75
Contemplation, detail

76
Contemplation, 1923
Marble, 104 cm
Meštrović Gallery, Split

77
Olga Meštrović, 1935
Marble, 58 cm
Meštrović Gallery, Split

78
Dancer, 1911
Marble, 96×50 cm
Meštrović Studio, Zagreb

79
Virgin and Child, 1925
Marble, 102 cm
Meštrović Gallery, Split

80
Virgin and Child, detail

81
Widow and Child, 1908
Marble
National Museum, Belgrade

82
Roman Pietà, 1942—1946
Marble
University of Notre Dame, South Bend

83
Roman Pietà, detail

84
Head of Moses, 1926
Marble, 120 cm
Bezalel Museum, Jerusalem

85
The Descent from the Cross
Wood
Tate Gallery, London

86
Christ and Mary Magdalene, 1916
Wood, 176×134 cm
Glyptotheca, Zagreb

87
In Gethsemane, 1940
Wood, 180×126 cm
Kaštelet, Split

88
Crucifixion, 1919
Wood, 330 cm
Kaštelet, Split

89
Crucifixion, detail, 1919
Wood, 330 cm
Kaštelet, Split

90
Head of Christ, 1911
Wood, 60 cm
Meštrović Gallery, Split

91
The Deposition, 1917
Wood, 173×130 cm
Kaštelet, Split

92
The Deposition, detail

93
The Expulsion from the Temple, detail

94
The Temptation, 1917
180×100 cm
Kaštelet, Split

95
The Raising of Lazarus, detail, 1943
Wood, 180×134 cm
Kaštelet, Split

96
The Raising of Lazarus, detail, 1943
Wood
Kaštelet, Split

97
Christ's Baptism, detail, 1953
Wood, 180×98 cm
Kaštelet, Split

98
The Ascension, detail, 1953
Wood
Kaštelet, Split

99
Christ and the Adulteress, detail, 1943
Wood
Kaštelet, Split

100
Christ and the Woman of Samaria, 1927
Wood, 180 × 112 cm
Kaštelet, Split

101
The Annunciation, 1927
Wood, 180 × 111 cm
Kaštelet, Split

102
Noli Me Tangere, detail, 1943
Wood
Kaštelet, Split

103
Christ and Mary Magdalene, detail

104
Resurrexit, 1943
Wood, 180 × 134 cm
Kaštelet, Split

105
Happy Angels, detail

106
Mother and Child, 1927
Wood, 135 cm
Meštrović Studio, Zagreb

107
Girl Plaiting her Hair, 1919
Wood, 88 × 47 cm
Meštrović Studio, Zagreb

108
Angel with a Flute, 1921
Wood, 141 cm
Meštrović Studio, Zagreb

109
Angel with a Flute, detail

110
Adam, 1941
Wood, 308 cm
Meštrović Gallery, Split

111
Caryatid, 1918
Wood, 188 cm
Meštrović Gallery, Split

112
Male Nude
Chalk, 64 × 45 cm
Meštrović Gallery, Split

113
Female Nude
Charcoal, 51 × 38.5 cm
Meštrović Gallery, Split

114
Prophet, 1925
Crayon drawing
Meštrović Gallery, Split

115
Orpheus
Chalk drawing
Owner unknown

116
Sad Angels, 1917
Wood, 122 × 82 cm
Meštrović Gallery, Split

117
Happy Angels, 1917
Wood, 117 × 83 cm
Meštrović Gallery, Split

118
Women from the Entry into Jerusalem
Wood, 177 × 37 cm
Meštrović Studio, Zagreb

119
Virgin and Child, 1917
Wood, 67 cm
Meštrović Studio, Zagreb

120
The Virgin and Angels, 1917
Wood, 173 × 124 cm
Kaštelet, Split

121
Resurrexit, 1941
Drawing
Meštrović Gallery, Split

122
**Study for Frescoes in the Meštrović Memorial
Chapel, Otavice,** 1938
Chalk, 64 × 45 cm
Meštrović Gallery, Split

123
Artist of my People, 1908
Bronze, 173 × 83 cm
Meštrović Gallery, Split

124
Woman's Torso, 1940
Marble, 92 cm
Meštrović Gallery, Split